DIME-STORE DREAM PARADE

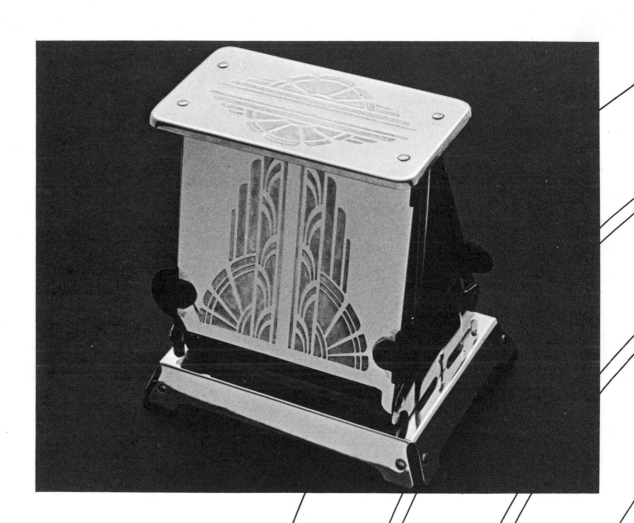

DIME~STORE DREAM PARADE

Popular Culture 1925-1955

Robert Heide and John Gilman

Photographs by Lawrence Otway

E. P. DUTTON ❦ NEW YORK

This book is lovingly dedicated to the memory of Robert's mother, Olga, who lived through these times and who in later years was a good friend to John.

ACKNOWLEDGMENTS

The authors wish to give thanks to Alexandra Anderson and to Robert Lesser for their initial encouragement of this project. Other influences on this book have included Grover Van Dexter of Second Childhood, New York; Howard Otway of Theatre 80 St. Marks, New York; Randolph Carter, the late Joe Cino, Lady Hope Stansbury, Andy Warhol, Ron Link, Warren Cresswell, Al Trommer, Tim Bissell, Ken Ketwig, and Lee Perrine.

The authors also are grateful for the contribution made by their editor, Cyril I. Nelson, without whose vision and guidance this book would not have been possible.

CONTENTS

ROBERT HEIDE grew up during the World War II era in Irvington, New Jersey. He received his education at Northwestern University and studied for the theatre with Stella Adler and Uta Hagen. As a New York–based playwright he has written *Hector,* produced at the Cherry Lane Theatre; *West of the Moon* at New Playwrights; *Why Tuesday Never Has a Blue Monday* at LaMama Experimental Theater; and *Moon* and *The Bed,* two off-off Broadway theatre classics, originally presented at the Caffe Cino. Recent plays include *American Hamburger,* presented at Theatre for the New City, and *Increased Occupancy* and *Suburban Tremens* produced by New York Theatre Strategy. His plays have been published in *The Best of Off-Off Broadway* (1969), *New American Plays Volume 4* (1971), *The Off-Off Broadway Book* (1972), and in acting editions. Robert Heide's feature articles have appeared in *The Village Voice, Soho Weekly News,* and *Other Stages.* He is also a collector of "fabulous artifacts" from the golden era of popular culture.

JOHN GILMAN was born in Honolulu, Hawaii. His father LaSelle Gilman is noted as the author of *The Red Gate, Shanghai Deadline, The Dragon's Mouth,* and other popular 1940s and 1950s adventure novels set in the Far East. John Gilman spent his childhood years in the Islands and later in Grosse Pointe, Michigan, and San Francisco, California, where he attended City College and majored in journalism. His varied career has included work as an actor, a radio disc jockey, and a stage manager. He held the position of Executive Secretary for the Association for Mentally Ill Children in New York and was also the Executive Director of the American Society of Magazine Photographers. An avid interest in Art Deco and nostalgia collectibles led Mr. Gilman to exhibit at the New York Art Deco Exposition at Radio City Music Hall and at the National Antiques Show at Madison Square Garden.

INTRODUCTION: GOOD TIMES ARE HERE TO STAY

Popular Culture and the Depression

The term *popular culture* most often stands for a certain set of stylizations, themes, and attitudes that apply specifically to what is appealing on a mass level during a given period in a society. This encompasses popular trends in fashion, functionalism, decorative styles and designs, modes of transportation, architecture, and developments in production and distribution —including communications systems and the arts. Popular culture is usually said to reflect the sociological, political, and economic factors of a society, but during periods of upheaval and crisis it has also existed as a catalyst that, reacting against predominant social conventions or taboos, presents itself as a new counterpoint in relation to the whole.

It is ironic that the most prolific and important period for new developments in popular culture was not the two world wars of this century, great as their impact was in affecting the course of cultural changes in the world, but was instead the Great Depression,

Button made by Walt Disney Enterprises to be given away at early screenings of *The Three Little Pigs*, 1933. © Walt Disney Productions.

which spanned only eight to ten years. The concept of a progressive modernism coexisting with depression and despair is the incongruous yet accurate analogy for this time. This dualism certainly applies to the years we are concerned with here, the era of the late industrial age—specifically, the thirty-year period in America from 1925 to 1955. The main focus of this study is on developments in the 1930s, with a consideration of some of the elements, movements, and fashions in the mid- to late 1920s that contributed to the dynamics of the 1930s. Visuals from the 1940s, the period of World War II, and the post-World War II era up to 1955 are included chiefly to provide a continuum of the styles deriving from early modernism.

The year 1955 is selected as the end of our inquiry because we see it as marking the beginning of the era of the cheap disposable, still a predominant force in our latter-day pop culture. As of 1955, quality and craftsmanship in design as well as in the materials used declined sharply because new manufacturing methods began to produce items of an inferior quality, due to the planned obsolescence of machinery, automobiles, and household appliances.

As we were investigating this early modern period, it became more and more apparent that it was the Great Depression that had the deepest effect on the specific changes that took place in our society in the sphere of modernist movements and American popular culture. The poverty, disillusionment, and despair of the Depression created a sharp break with many outmoded theories, conventions, and social structures that had been dominant since the 1900s. Political and economic factors, replacing the old ideologies, forced people to examine and explore new, sometimes radical, alternatives. Ultimately, it appears that the old and the new met in compromise, and there is no doubt that in 1930s America modernity became firmly established through great changes in conventions, morals, attitudes, and styles.

The walls of provincial thinking appeared to collapse alongside the stock market crash on Wall Street, ultimately to be supplanted with more sophisticated ideas advanced through the new modern cultural mediums—radio and motion pictures. Radio opened up communications channels from large cities to small towns and farm areas, just as the movies created new ideas of glamour, fantasy, and the good life for everybody. Certainly the radio and moving-picture industries were a phenomenal thrust forward culturally in the 1920s, but it was the technical advancements made in mass-production mechanical systems that marked the 1930s as the technological "zenith" of the modern age.

The origin of the Great Depression can be discerned prior to World War I. Newspapers and periodicals of the day describing the economic crash called it the inevitable result of industrial revolution. The machine as a monster intent on consuming its creator, eliminating the worker, and possibly devouring all mankind was a popular theme in books and films in the late 1920s and 1930s. The confrontation of man and machine is depicted in Fritz Lang's powerful German silent film *Metropolis* (1926), in which masses of men are intent on finding a humanistic relationship to a vast machine complex, whose only purpose seems to be continuous, repetitious, and indifferent production. *Metropolis* presented a dream-projection to the year 2000; but clearly the point was the destructive potential in the machine and the serious danger of men losing their identities. John and Ruth Vassos, in their prophetic books, *Contempo* (1929), *Ultimo* (1930), and *Humanities* (1935), portrayed this unquiet future in text and stylized modern drawings, as did Stuart Chase in *Men and Machines* (1929). Yet fear of the machine did not mean it lacked a fascinated public. Machines were considered the key to the new modern age, for machinery ultimately could make real the radiant new utopian cities like those envisioned by Le Corbusier. No doubt the machine in the late industrial age had made incredible technological leaps. The automobile had come into its own, and the fascination with air travel, the airplane, and the zeppelin was worldwide.

C. A. Glasgold in his essay "Design in America," from the book *Modern American Design* (1930), had this to say:

> *We see ourselves immersed in a mechanical civilization and we fear lest the values of life be submerged beneath the inhuman weight of the machine. In some, this fear has tended to provoke a vigorous condemnation of the machine age and to arouse a nostalgic, yet vain longing for "the good old days." Nevertheless we must accept contemporary conditions. It is utterly impossible to undo what has already been accomplished by Taut, Le Corbusier, Van Der Rohe, Wright, Gropius, and others. Besides, and what is more important, by the exercise of intelligence we can force the machine into the service of beauty.*

Machine dominance certainly was one factor in the collapse of the stock market, although on Black Thursday, October 24, 1929, it was money and the banks that were the main concerns of many Americans who angrily sought causes for this disaster. With the official closing of banks followed by massive unemployment, one interpretation followed another in furthering confusion and disbelief. Production lines replacing individual craftsmen in scores of factories and small shops, machines operating at five times the capacity of a worker and with more dexterity, food-

Two issues of a Depression-era magazine promoting salesmanship, 1932.

processing plants employing machinery that revolutionized the corner grocery store and reinterpreted the role of farming, electricity as energy increasing productivity—all of these contributed to the overproduction that steadily weakened the economy and led to a saturation point.

The fear of every middle-class worker and his family in the early 1930s was the breadline. During the peak years of the Depression (1932–1933) 12 to 15 million men were unemployed. This meant that 25 to 30 million more—families, men, women, and children—stood in breadlines, milklines, and ate in soup kitchens at one time or another. Many were fed in municipal lodgings, or at the Salvation Army, and lived in Federal Emergency Relief camps, transient shelters, vacant lots, and parks. Charities formed to offer food to the needy; and at 5 & 10¢ Depression restaurants established for the unemployed you could obtain a 6¢ lunch that might include one egg, a dish of baked beans, a bowl of soup, a doughnut, and a cup of coffee. For those lucky enough to find work with an average weekly pay of $15.00, a home or apartment could be rented at $7.00 per month. Mothers had to learn about budgeting household expenses, and with little money in circulation, store prices were eventually forced down. Families might use no more than a 25-watt light bulb for evening reading, for energy was seen as an expensive commodity; and home sewing was a necessity in order to keep clothing in steady repair. Whistling happy Depression songs in the Bing Crosby manner, like "Keep Your Sunny Side Up," "Let's Have Another Cup of Coffee, Let's Have Another Piece of Pie," or "I Found a Million Dollar Baby in the Five and Ten Cent Store" and sustaining a cheerful facade gave people the courage to feel they could chase that persistent wolf (sometimes a euphemism for the landlord) from the back door. "Who's Afraid of the Big Bad Wolf" from Walt Disney's popular Silly Symphony cartoon *The Three Little Pigs* became a theme song for the Depression. Adults and children could readily identify with the plight of the frightened little pigs and their frenetic search for security.

Advertisements from 1930s household or ladies' magazines depicting brightly colored gelatin concoctions set in molds shaped into ornate pyramids imply that this would make a meal along with a bowl of Campbell's or Heinz 57 Varieties' canned soups. Farina, Shredded Ralston, Post Toasties, or Mello-Wheat at 15¢ to 18¢ a box kept Junior satisfied in the morning, especially if a Tom Mix or G-Man premium was included in the box—followed by Ovaltine, the pep-up chocolate energy drink mixed in his colorful Orphan Annie Beetleware shake-up mug. The main image presented by periodicals was the American family, the backbone of the nation and pivotal theme for all social and ethical beliefs. Dad was pictured reading the want ads in his easy chair, smoking a Chesterfield, Lucky Strike, or Camel cigarette, while mother seemed happy enough doing her weekly wash in Rinso White. Blondie and Dagwood, Chic Young's famous comic-strip characters, represented the typical struggling middle-class American family of the Depression. They lived in a one-family suburban home on Shady Lane Avenue with their son Baby Dumpling (later called Alexander), daughter Cookie, and pet dog Daisy. Dagwood was a persistent bungler constantly being fired and rehired by his irate boss Mr. Dithers. Late-night, oversized "Dagwood" sandwiches temporarily assuaged his frustrations while his distracted marcelled-blonde wife mindlessly spent their hard-earned money on chic little hats and frocks.

Maggie and Jiggs, comic characters created by George McManus, best symbolized the excesses and foibles of a wealthier class. Maggie consistently chased after Jiggs with a rolling pin, throwing him out of the house after he accidentally smashed one of

Sheet music for "Who's Afraid of the Big Bad Wolf" (1933), the theme song of the Depression. © Walt Disney Productions.

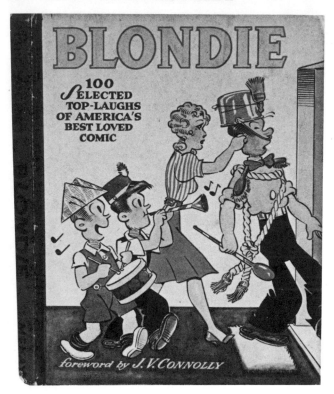

The escapades of the Dagwood Bumstead family, created by Chic Young and published by David McKay Co., 1944.

her expensive Art Deco vases. Advertisements depicted the upper-class men in tuxedos and top hats, and their ladies in sleek satin gowns, entering a new 1934 twelve-cylinder, four-door, $6,700 Packard on their way to the opera, the theatre, or to nightclub high jinks. A Packard car advertising slogan "for a discriminating clientele" made the point that this was not a vehicle to be purchased by anyone, just as *Vanity Fair*, *Vogue*, and *Harper's Bazaar* magazines catered to either a moneyed or an intellectual elite with little or no interest in the plight of middle-class Americans. In these periodicals references to the Depression were somehow consistently and conspicuously omitted.

During the bleak winter of 1932/33, changes, signposts of "good times to come," appeared to be on the horizon. Franklin D. Roosevelt was elected President; and a couple of months later, on December 5, 1933, National Prohibition, known also as the Volstead Act, in existence since January 16, 1920, was repealed. In 1925 there had been over 100,000 speakeasies serving liquor in New York City alone, not to mention the nearby city of Hoboken, which was tagged the "one-mile-square gin mill." In any case, many people had been brewing their own wine or beer in their cellars, which usually doubled as the family hideaway barroom. By 1934, with repeal, the cocktail

lounge and Moderne chromium cocktail shaker came openly into their own as status symbols of a new sophistication, glamour, and independence for 1930s America, and bars suddenly reappeared on every corner in every town, many new, some reopened.

On Saturday, March 4, 1933, millions of Americans huddled around the radio listening to Roosevelt's inaugural address: "This great nation will endure as it has endured, will revive and prosper . . . so first let me assert my firm belief that the only thing we have to fear is fear itself . . . nameless, unjustified terror which paralyzes needed effort to convert retreat into advance . . . ," bringing words of prayer

Promotional button from Dunlop Tire & Rubber Co., 1933.

Ronson chrome and Bakelite table lighter with two side compartments for cigarettes, c. 1934.

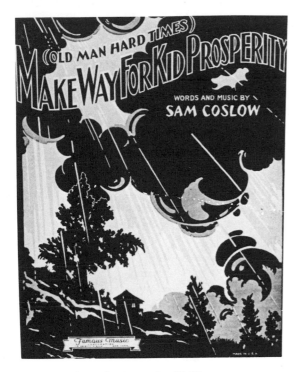

Depression sheet music, 1930.

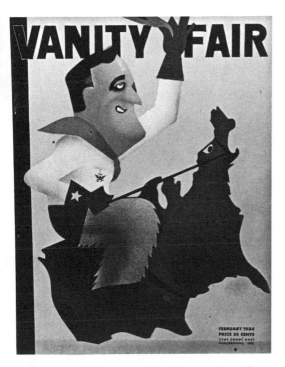

Franklin D. Roosevelt caricatured on the cover of *Vanity Fair*, February 1934.

and hope in a forceful tone to a populace that had become despondent and desperate. Roosevelt with his famous fireside chats on the radio was proclaimed a hero symbolic of a new forward-looking posture for Americans. Roosevelt's innovative "New Deal," which lasted from 1933 to 1940, did not immediately remove the gloom of the Depression, but it did alleviate the fear of it by instituting morale-building programs like the National Recovery Act, which created "codes of fair competition" among businessmen and set maximum hours of labor and new minimum-wage levels. The NRA, symbolized by the famous "Blue Eagle" seen in every factory and shopwindow during the Depression, stamped on every pound of butter or ton of coal, on magazines and newspapers and in movie credits and newsreels, gave the entire country the opportunity to participate in the nation's recovery with its prideful slogan "We Do Our Part." The Works Progress Administration (WPA) had a profound effect on the development of new ideas and changing styles; its hundreds of individual projects, employing artists, designers, builders, and craftsmen, marked the first time the American government took direct action in shaping the popular taste on a national level. The Federal Emergency Relief Administration put over $20 billion in wages and relief payments into the hands of those in need and able to work, changing the song of the day from "Brother Can You Spare a Dime?" to "Make Way for Kid Prosperity."

Glass and chromium cocktail tray with Art Deco motif reverse-painted in red, black, and cream, c. 1930.

Modernism Comes to America

Innovations in modern decorative styles originating in the 1920s swept into the 1930s with the force of a monsoon. A dissatisfaction with the conventional dark-wood, bric-a-brac German Humperdinck or Gingerbread rococo forms so predominant after the turn of the century in the majority of middle-class homes caused many designers to look to "modernism" as the alternative to these outmoded ornamentations. The strongest influence on the American modernists came out of the Bauhaus, which had originally revolutionized design in Europe in the early 1920s by providing new technics and models for industry. In 1925 the Bauhaus collective moved to prestigious new headquarters in Dessau, designed by Walter Gropius, who founded the German modernist movement in Weimar in 1919 and was its chief director until 1928. Emigrating to the United States in 1937, Gropius became chairman of the architecture department in the Graduate School of Design at Harvard, while continuing to design advanced modern structures in America. By the early 1930s the Bauhaus maintained a steady influence on artisans and designers under the leadership of Hannes Meyer, Ludwig Mies van der Rohe, Richard Neutra, and Walter Gropius. Gropius, in particular, developed futuristic design techniques similar to the advanced housing estates exhibited at Weissenhof in Stuttgart in 1927 that had integrated prefabricated units into new concepts of urbanism offering dream-city housing plans for living in the modern age.

Adolf Hitler vehemently opposed the Bauhaus, since he had a sentimental preference for the more traditional architectural forms, even though he borrowed readily from the movement's modern design theories and techniques to promote his Nazi party's image. A black swastika in a white circle on a red background is pure Bauhaus, with roots also traceable back to American Indian pure-line geometric symbolism. The Bauhaus, it should be noted, had scant interest in the forms and patterns being created by the French Art Deco movement of the mid-1920s, since it objected to the exotic, curvilinear motifs being used in conjunction with the more elemental rectilinear and functional ones. The strict, formal Bauhaus image advocated all things mechanistic and it was the Bauhaus's postulate that modern art and design movements ought to incorporate and aid the evolution of machine technology.

The term *Art Deco,* widely employed today to cover some of the cross-current movements prevalent during the early modern period, is an abbreviation made from the 1925 Paris Exposition Internationale des Arts Décoratifs et Industriels Modernes, an exhibition that included everything in the industrial and

Cover of *House Beautiful* magazine illustrating a Moderne interior, October 1935.

Large, white pottery vase with hand-sculpted bas-relief, signed Nagy, c. 1927.

Industrial Moderne electric clock in chromium-plated zinc, designed by Gilbert Rohde and made by the Herman Miller Clock Co. Introduced at Chicago's "Century of Progress" exhibition, 1934.

French Art Deco table clock in blue terra-cotta, 1925.

decorative arts from architecture to fashion. Although not fully representative of modernism, in that the Dutch De Stijl and the Bauhaus were noticeably excluded, this exposition was and still remains an important key to modern styles developed in the twentieth century. Art Deco, also referred to as Art Moderne in the 1930s, can be traced back as early as 1910 with influences drawn from the Ballets Russes in Paris and the modernist Oriental designs of Leon Bakst. Cubism, Expressionism, and Futurism, in particular, the works of Wassily Kandinsky, Pablo Picasso, Georges Braque, and Henri Matisse, preceded and contributed to Art Deco as a formal style as did the Wiener Werkstätte of Vienna as well as the Deutscher Werkbund. Other early influences are the Aztec and Mayan cultures, African tribal designs, and the 1920s vogue for dapper, stylized American and English black jazz bands. Large tropical leaf patterns, exotic flowers, jungle birds, and Zulu masks were readily incorporated from primitive cultures into modern decoration. The opening of Tutankhamen's tomb in 1922 created a fad for reinterpretations of the ancient Egyptian pyramid, sphinx heads, elongated cats, and geometric ziggurat progressions.

By the 1930s *modernism* was no longer just an avant-garde term, having survived the capriciousness of a public who initially reacted with resistance, attempting to relegate the new movements into the domain of the "oddball" or "quirky." The popular Paris Exposition left an indelible impression on archi-

tecture, domestic interior design, consumer goods, and packaging and introduced to the world a format for a new civilized and "modern" way of life. The exhibition also marked the formal early rumblings of the union between art and industry—man and machine—influencing everything modern from that time until today. The prevalent style exhibited was geometric with an overlay of the "French manner"; but as early as 1928 there were already signs of decline in the more romantic inclinations of Art Deco. Large cabbage roses, flowers arranged in baskets, languishing nudes, leaping gazelles, tiered fountains, and similar extravagant decorative motifs began to wane as a more austere linear style that was the quintessence of the industrial Bauhaus came into favor. Cubistic angularity later replaced the Art Nouveau influence of the curvilinear in Art Deco. Lightning bolts, sunrays, running borzois or whippets, autos, airplanes, locomotives, exaggerated figurines of women in motion with Moderne, masklike features and hair flying in zigzag progression, and any number of symbols representing the dynamics of speed and acceleration were the new "pur et simple" design motifs.

In 1925 little or no modern commercial design existed in America, which retained an attitude that was culturally isolated even after World War I; so that when President Herbert Hoover was asked to contribute to the Paris Exposition he had to decline, stating that America could offer little or nothing in the area of modern decorative arts. The handful of

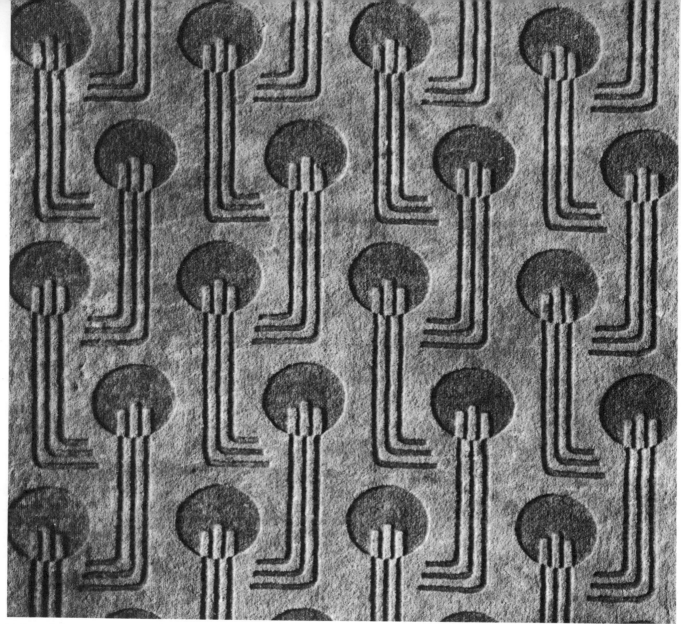

Mohair fabric in a russet circular pattern against a pearl-gray background that was used as a "tidy-cover" for a standing Victrola, c. 1928. Photograph by Helga Photo Studio.

Industrial-design, streamlined pop-up electric toaster (Model T-9) made by Sunbeam, Chicago, Illinois, c. 1938.

Embossed-leather card case, c. 1929.

department store buyers and interior and textile designers returning to the States from the exposition were eager to bring back with them its new modern-design concepts. In 1928 both Lord & Taylor and Macy's held separate special New York showings of modern interiors, introducing modernism as a viable commodity for the city apartment or the suburban home. Macy's "Art in Trade Exposition" exhibited special rooms in the Art Deco-Art Moderne style featuring an international collective that included French designers Leleu and Dufrene, the Germans Bruno Paul and Kem Weber, who was by then also designing Hollywood sets, the Austrian Josef Hoffman and the Italian Gio Ponti. Macy's presentation was sponsored by The Metropolitan Museum of Art, who held their own show entitled "The Architect and the Industrial Arts" (1929) with room interiors by Joseph Urban and Eliel Saarinen. A number of artifacts, including furniture by Jacques Emile Ruhlmann had been purchased for The Metropolitan in Paris. A similar exhibition at the museum in 1934 introduced the newer influences, namely the emergence of the Bauhaus, as well as the economic impact the Depression was having on industry, which prompted new designers to create simpler solutions to design problems. Lee Simonson, Raymond Loewy, and William Lescaze created spare interiors, using only those materials and forms that could be reproduced economically on a mass scale by craftsmen of average skills.

Another important exhibition called "Machine Art" (1934) was also held in New York by The Museum of Modern Art, which showed a wide range of new manufactures such as kitchen utility items, bathroom plumbing fixtures, and ordinary hardware implements—presenting them as "art" for the first time. In the design magazine *Arts and Decoration*, industrial designer Walter Dorwin Teague commented in 1936: "Painting and sculpture are art but so is the making of kitchen sinks and pickle bottles."

Industrial design developed in 1930s America in much the same way as ecological-energy movements persist today. There was both public resistance and attraction to the newfangled gadgetry and the feeling of necessity that comes from what appears inevitable. There seemed to be no way of avoiding these new designers who maneuvered their aesthetic into every corner of society. Traditional crafts began to be assimilated by the machine, and materials such as aluminum, bent tubular steel, textiles, wood, linoleum, glass, and marble could be dealt with more efficiently through mass production. Machine-produced synthetics such as Formica, Bakelite, Celluloid, Catalin, Tenite, Plaskon, Beetleware, Lucite, and other plastics came out of the factory to be incorporated into dishes, knives and forks, jewelry, radio cabinets, and

a hundred other household and commercial items. Industrial designers united with engineers, chemists, market researchers, economists, scientists, fashion experts, and other specialists in an effort to improve products. Designs had to be ultramodernized but practical, with their outward appearance corresponding to performance, function, and commercialism. In the early 1930s designers like Paul Frankl, Walter von Nessen, Raymond Loewy, Henry Dreyfuss, Norman Bel Geddes, and Gilbert Rohde stunned America with their imaginative drive and modernist design techniques, which began to be used with increased regularity by manufacturers. These men and scores of others streamlined everything from airplanes to toasters, including furniture, lighting fixtures, telephones, alarm clocks, automobiles, ships, trains, and waffle irons, creating a new, growing consumer ethic in the middle of the Depression. Americans were quick to appreciate this new modernism in the marketplace, and professionals in every field enthusiastically redecorated their offices, beauty parlors, and stores in Industrial Art Moderne.

Flexible red-and-white Bakelite case with individual cigarette compartments shown with its original box, 1935.

Industrial-design chair made for beauty parlors, offices, restaurants, and the home. Chrome and leatherette design for Modernage, Inc., c. 1935.

1.
FIVE-AND-DIME MEMORY BANK

Furnishing the Depression Home

MEMORY IMAGE: *The boy is in knickers, wearing a gray-and-maroon plaid mackinaw topped by a tweed cap pulled tightly over Vaseline-slicked hair. Accompanied by his mother, a stout woman dressed in a fitted, ankle-length pea-green woolen coat with a fluffy red-fox fur collar, a small veiled hat and black cotton gloves, he jumps aboard the downtown trolley; their destinations this wintry day in 1932 are the department stores and the five-and-dimes. Mother dreams of household appliances, rugs, knickknacks, or a new lamp for the living room, while Junior, restless and fidgety, anxiously anticipates his visit to the toy department and a Woolworth luncheon counter where he can order his favorite noontime snack, a hot dog smeared with yellow mustard and an orange soda. Screeching loudly to a halt at an intersection, the trolley picks up more passengers, giving Mother a moment to catch a glimpse of the grocery display with painted advertising price-list signs in an A&P window and to scrutinize her Depression budget book to see what the family can afford to eat this week.*

A&P food prices, examined from today's viewpoint, would be like a whirligig trip into the upsidedown world of Oz: Wildmere eggs were 29¢ a dozen, a quart of milk was 10¢, a pound of butter 28¢, a two-pound package of Red Circle Coffee could be bought for 35¢, Bokar, the "better coffee in a tin," was 23¢ a pound, a box of Ritz Crackers 17¢, a large bottle of College Inn Tomato Juice 15¢, a two-pound can of Broadcast Corn Beef Hash 23¢, tomatoes were three pounds for 17¢, Palmolive Soap sold at 12 bars for 49¢, a twenty-four-ounce-size tin of Log Cabin Syrup for 25¢, and Jello or puddings were four packages for 15¢.

Other than food chains, the main consumer outlets for the average middle-class family of the Depression period up through the mid-1950s were the department stores, large variety chains, and the five-and-dimes. Five-and-ten-cent stores—F. W. Woolworth, S. S. Kresge, S. H. Kress, J. J. Newberry, McCrory's, and H. L. Green—were the ultimate chain stores that created new merchandising methods for buying and selling, offering something for everyone. In 1929 the Woolworth chain had 2,100 stores in America and abroad. Established in 1879, Woolworth advertised "amazing buying opportunities for your

Household budget ledger, c. 1931.

Red-and-brown, snap-cap syrup tins made by The Log Cabin Products Co., 1940s.

nickels and dimes." Woolworth officials described their credo in a company periodical:

Through the humble agencies of nickels and dimes, F. W. Woolworth has multiplied the possibilities of home beauty and home efficiency and has extended the standards of living in a score of directions. Its place in the home-making of America is not only the most intimate of any mercantile institution but the most far reaching. More than ten million customers are served at its counters each shopping day.

This was written according to the gospel of salesmanship in the year of the crash, and by 1933, four years later, Woolworth had added 395 stores to its chain. Despite the Depression, Woolworth continued opening stores and multiplying customers, selling a wide assortment of items from lipstick and candy to records and sheet music. You name it and you could find it at the five-and-dime. Advertising "nothing over 10¢," Woolworth and other dime stores eventually went from "5 & 10¢" to "5¢ 10¢ & $1."

American department stores such as R. H. Macy's, L. Bamberger's, John Wanamaker, Gimbel's, Bloomingdale's, Hahnes & Company, B. Altman, Lord & Taylor, Stern's and Marshall Field set trends and styles in fashion and introduced new concepts for modern living in the 1930s in conjunction with their standard, contemporary or "traditional" categories. Modern furniture in bent tubular chrome, coffee or cocktail tables with black glass or lacquered tops, stylized and streamlined club chairs or black-and-chromium torchère floor lamps were featured in many

Candy tin originally sold at Woolworth's five-and-dime in 1928.

Torchère floor lamp, chrome and black enamel, c. 1928.

A Moderne 1930s sunroom with torchère floor lamps, upholstered, tubular-chrome chairs, chrome tables with black lacquer tops, a green-and-blue Scotch plaid rug, modishly painted deep royal-blue walls and ceilings, and chartreuse accents. Illustrated in *Homefurnishing Arts,* Spring and Summer 1935.

model room displays and caused a stir among customers; but most often this type of furniture was still primarily consigned to specialty designer outlets.

In the traditional line, beaded or fringed floor or bridge lamps were selling for $7.95 up in the home furnishings department and enjoyed great popularity in the 1920s and 1930s with housewives and decorators. Used to achieve warmth and softness in a living room setting or boudoir, these exotic lamps with shades of hand-painted stretched silk or glazed parchment still retained an inescapable association with the ornate decor found in a brothel or showgirl's gilded pied-à-terre.

Since father had little time for divertisement from his role as breadwinner and home repairman, mother became the interior decorator. Decorative interior color schemes used in the middle-class Depression home customarily emphasized maroon, cream, dark green, mauve, tan, mulberry, slate, mallow pink, or delphinium blue. Living or bedroom draperies, wallpaper, linoleum, and rug patterns incorporated flowers and leaves like the rambler rose, hydrangea, chrysanthemum, and sometimes employed striking Bauhaus or Art Deco angular block progressions. Mirrored glass-top coffee and cocktail tables became a vogue throughout the period; cobalt blue was the most common variety, but peach-colored mirror was also popular. Decorators sometimes suggested chartreuse, rose, and gold mirror for the more

modern-minded customer, but mother preferred blue glass available in a variety of intensities. Large round wall mirrors, cabinets, Moderne-style false fireplace fronts, knickknack shelves, and centerpiece table mirrors were all "mirrored in color," often mixed in a grandiose manner, blue with white, or peach with blue, occasionally employing frosted and etched designs of wild birds or ships. Bold geometric or circular Art Deco patterns painted on mirrorized glass with black, maroon, green, or red enamel were another popular trend for decorative trays, wall mirrors, and 1930s easel picture frames. The "cobalt" used to make the blue mirror turned out to be a special substance that was needed by the government in the late 1940s for producing atom bombs; and, consequently, its decorative uses were discontinued.

The typical middle-class living-room set found in the furniture department consisted of a sofa in plain or patterned rich maroon or rose velour with one medium-size chair (usually mother's) done to match the three-cushion sofa, while the other larger, easy chair, often referred to as "a Bumstead" after the kind Dagwood fell into with his evening paper, would be a deep royal blue or vibrant green. Slipcovers were a Depression must, reducing wear and tear on the furniture, and the fabrics available for them were in brightly colored vat-dyed floral prints of cabbage roses, rhododendrons, magnolia blossoms, gardenias, bamboo, and tropical palm leaf patterns. These plush, overstuffed three-piece sets, sometimes

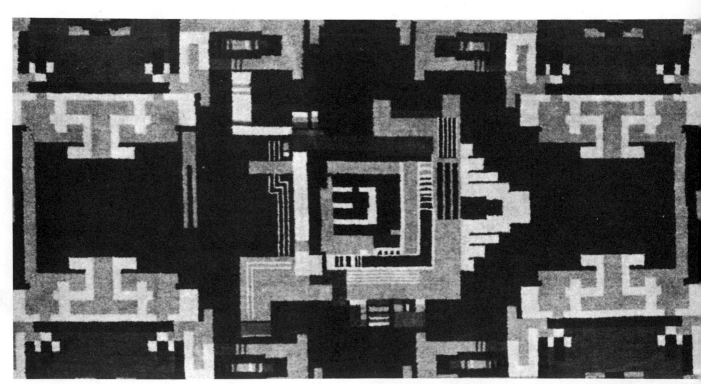

Geometric patterned rug in various shades of brown, 1930s.

including an ottoman, could be purchased for $79.50, with an easy payment plan of $5.00 down and $5.00 a month. Wicker furniture enameled in coffee brown, cream, Saxon green, tangerine, or Indian yellow often graced the sun parlor or front porch. A wicker davenport cost $18.95 and a wicker rocker was $7.55. The family dining-room set, a hardwood table with five chairs, could be bought for $27.95, while for sleep a bedstead, spring, and mattress was $21.98 complete. A modernistic Grand Rapids bedroom set featuring inlaid Oriental and buff walnut veneers, Bakelite knobs with blue-mirror decorative accents, consisting of a vanity with an oversize circular mirror, a double head- and footboard, a wardrobe, a chest, and a dresser sold for a low $49.95.

Novelty mood lamps became status symbols in many homes of the 1930s along with ornate mantel clocks, both of which used dramatic and often outré Art Deco motifs. Frankart, Inc., was a small factory in New York City that produced and marketed thousands of specialty items for distribution in department stores and better gift shops. Clocks, lamps, ashtrays, cigarette boxes, candy containers, stylized fishbowl stands, bookends, vases, candle holders, floor ashtrays, and coffee tables, which used one or more nude statuettes in spray-painted gunmetal, black enamel, and Depression green, a patina meant to represent aged bronze or copper, were first individually created in sculpture from "real life" models and then formed into molds by the company's president/

Metal scrap basket with
Art Deco floral motif, c. 1926.

Easel picture frame decorated in black, cream, and silver with a photograph of Shirley Temple, c. 1936.

Streamlined, overstuffed club chair in rose mohair, c. 1937. Photograph by Tim Bissell.

Magenta and Nile green palm print on vat-dyed cotton upholstery and drapery fabric, c. 1938. Photograph by Helga Photo Studio.

art director, Arthur von Frankenberg. Nudes, with arms reaching upward as if in reverence to the sun à la Isadora Duncan, gazing into Mazdalite encased in gold-, pink-, or lime-frosted crackle-glass globes, became the symbols for an era fascinated by electricity. Frankart's facial features, hands, and feet were not detailed in the manner of the chryselephantine bronze-ivory sculptures of Dimitri Chiparus or F. Priess, since the cheaper Frankart pieces were mainly silhouette shadow lamps for decorative accent. The expression "Dancing Lady" was applied to these white French metal or lead sculpture pieces since they were meant to suggest the image of the showgirls seen in the Ziegfeld Follies or Earl Carroll Vanities. These American mass-produced items were modeled after earlier renderings of French "greenie"-style lamps created primarily by Max LeVerrier that originally were sold in Primavera, an exclusive designer shop in Paris. Other similar types of Deco figurines were made by the French artists Lorenzl, Limousin, Font, Fayral, or le Faguays, always in a sophisticated, dancing-in-motion frieze epitomizing the exuberance and modern attitudes the liberated woman was beginning to assimilate. A Frankart standing-lady ashtray from L. & C. Mayers, Inc., 1933 merchandise catalogue sold for $14.00, a Frankart dinner gong with nude was $7.00, "greenie" bookends were $4.00, and a shadow-globe lamp was $13.50, with over 170 variations of these individually molded pieces offered in separate 1927–1929 Frankart catalogues. The Nu-Art Company competed with Frank-

Twin "greenie" lamp with large crackle-glass globe, labeled Frankart, c. 1927.

Reclining Egyptian-style nude holding crackle-glass lamp, white metal with green-bronze patina on marble base, made by Max LeVerrier, 1930.

art, Inc., but their figurines did not exhibit the anatomical perfection of the Frankart forms. If you watch the Busby Berkeley films *Gold Diggers of 1933*, *Dames* (1933), or *Footlight Parade* (1933) closely you will notice a Frankart "greenie" on a mirrorized coffee table, vanity, or nightstand in Ruby Keeler's or Joan Blondell's apartment. Other statuary items in the Art Deco showgirl style found in department stores of 1933 might range in price from $25.00 to $100 depending on whether they were molded in bronze, silver, or pot metal; what type of base was used—marble, alabaster, or onyx; and also on the name of the artist or manufacturer.

Tropical fish, jungle birds like parrots, cockatoos, cranes, or flamingos; dogs such as the borzoi, greyhound, or whippet accompanied by glamorous ladies in picture hats; German shepherds, inspired by movie dogs Strongheart and Rin Tin Tin; Kerry blues; the popular Boston bull terrier; the Scottie named Fala owned by President Roosevelt; or the wirehaired terrier Asta, dog star of the "Thin Man" films, appeared in the form of cast-iron doorstops and as decorations on glasses, ashtrays, serving trays, bowls, metal boxes, and canisters. Arctic motifs, polar bear, and seal, and after Admiral Byrd's trip to the South Pole, the penguin; and panthers, lions, horses, camels, puffed-up doves, turkeys, or pigeons were prominent subjects appealing to a middle-class sensibility. Japan-ware, called *Noritake*, was also sold in the five-and-dimes in the 1930s in great volume, including hand-painted colorful flower vases, incense burners, tiny glass figures,

Combination ashtray and cigarette box in green milk glass with painted, stylized nude marked Frankart, c. 1930.

"Florida Deco" print of cranes in a mirrored frame, 1940.

pitchers, pincushions, planters, and other knickknacks for mother's shelves and windowsills.

Modern specialty pieces that added a dash of elegance to the Depression home were the post-Prohibition cocktail shakers, coffee servers, candy dishes, and buffet sets wrought in bright, gleaming electroplated chrome, copper, and brass with Catalin and Bakelite accents, created by industrial designers for the Chase Brass and Copper Company and the Manning Bowman Company, the leading manufacturers in this field.

Mother's Breadline Kitchen

The kitchen was painted Depression green (a medium Nile-gray green), French blue, or deep cream. Occasionally, a daring housewife would choose cardinal red or sunshine yellow; but the use of these brighter shades in kitchens did not really catch on until the 1940s. Armstrong Linoleum in brick squares or in bright Mondrian-like patterns inlaid on floors became a necessity in every modern kitchen. New machinery such as the monitor-top G. E. refrigerators, pop-up electric toasters, and electric mixers were a boon to mother in her "breadline kitchen," bringing "electrical modernism" directly into the home for the first time. An enamel stove purchased from the department store for $49.50 in the Depression stood next to a golden-oak hutch costing $29.95. The kitchen hutch or larder was an all-purpose cabinet with a porcelain work counter, tin-lined bread drawers, flour bin, flour sifter, and spice shelves usually complete with coffee and condiment jars. It often was enameled white or Depression green with decorative decal appliqués from Woolworth's of Dutch girls holding tulips, Mexicans, cacti, or Scotch terriers transferred onto the door panels. Ubiquitous in America was the sliding-leaf kitchen-table with four matching chairs; table frames and chair legs were made of wood or bent tubular chrome with the "antiseptic" porcelain tops decorated in horizontal, diagonal, geometric, or floral patterns.

Big cookie jars were the fun pop item to be found in the kitchens of the 1930s through the 1950s. Aunt Jemima Pancakes put out an entire set of cookie jars, saltshakers, syrup dispensers, measuring cups, notepad holders, and recipe containers with the Aunt Jemima image molded in bright red and yellow plastic. Every housewife knew that a Southern mammy was

(*above*). French silver-plated-bronze fish on onyx base, signed M. Font, c. 1928.

(*below*). Combination ashtray and end table made by the Chase Brass and Copper Company, chrome on brass with red leatherette, c. 1935. Photograph by Tim Bissell.

the ultimate cook, and these sets were a reminder of the old South's traditional kitchens. The Nelson McCoy Pottery Company produced many bizarre cookie jars and modeled one after Hattie MacDaniel who was featured in the film version of *Showboat* (1936) and played the unforgettable Mammy in *Gone with the Wind* (1939). Clowns, pelicans, and penguins were the subjects for cookie jars by McCoy; and other companies produced unusual double-faced "Siamese twin" comic-character cookie jars—Mickey Mouse on one side with Minnie on the other, Donald Duck with José Carioca, or Dumbo with Pluto.

Depression glass, also called *tank* glass, must have found its way into every kitchen in the 1920s, but not in the vast quantities and numbers of patterns that were offered to housewives by the 1930s. This glass, much sought after by collectors today, originally sold from 3¢ to 99¢ apiece, depending on quality and design. Five-and-dimes such as Woolworth, S. S. Kresge, or Kress sold four place settings (twenty pieces) for $1.99. Montgomery Ward in 1936 offered pink "Miss America" Depression glass, (twenty-two

(*above*). Tubular-chrome, kitchen barstool with leatherette top, c. 1940.

(*above, left*). "Turnover" toaster with Art Deco fountain motif, Westinghouse Electric Manufacturing Co., c. 1927.

(*left*). General Electric monitor-top, white-enamel refrigerator, 1931.

Left to right in back row: "Hattie McDaniel" cookie jar made by Nelson McCoy Pottery Company; red plastic Aunt Jemima cookie jar; ceramic Mammy cookie jar. *Middle row:* salt and pepper shakers. *Front row:* Aunt Jemima syrup dispenser, a sendaway from Aunt Jemima Pancakes, c. 1940.

Clown cookie jar made by Nelson McCoy Pottery Company, c. 1943.

Covered cookie jar and jug, "Mexicana" pattern, made by Fiesta Kitchen Kraft, c. 1939.

pieces) at a low $1.35, and a forty-four-piece blue luncheon set was only $2.98. Extra tumblers were 3¢ each. Attractive color was the main feature of this glass, and beautiful ambers, yellows, pinks, cobalt blues, burgundys, amethysts, and a wide variety of green tones made it a popular item that helped to brighten the bleak Depression days. Green glass was the most prevalent, and it was handed out as premiums in movie theatres, gas stations, and furniture stores to attract business. Food and soap products also included this type of giveaway in their promotional campaigns. A cobalt-blue milk pitcher, cereal bowl, and milk mug with a photolithograph of Shirley Temple embossed in white was offered with General Mills cereals at the local A&P; and everyone remembers Depression Giveaway Dish Night at the Rialto or Ritz.

Fiesta ware, designed by an Englishman named Frederick Rhead for the Homer-Laughlin China Company of Newell, West Virginia, was first produced in 1936; it featured in its original roster of five colors brilliant orange-red, dark blue, medium green, yellow, and ivory, colors skillfully blended to mix and match easily into one set, such as a red cup on a blue saucer, with a yellow cake plate next to a green teapot. After the Laughlin Company replaced antiquated dipping tubs with high-speed conveyor belts and automated spray-glazing, it could produce 30,000 dozen pieces of Fiesta dinnerware every day, thus meeting the increased demand. Fiesta ware was sold mainly in department or better stores, although three cheaper but equally colorful lines in different design patterns were created especially for sale at the five-and-dimes. Harlequin was sold exclusively through Woolworth, and a line called Tango through J. J. Newberry. Another cheaper dime-store variety was Riviera. The

Small pottery teapot, Japan, 1935.

Art Deco–patterned cover for a bridge scorepad, c. 1930.

Elegant modern china (made in Japan) that was sold at Woolworth's in either blue or sepia tones, c. 1930.

better type of Fiesta pottery sold seventy-six pieces for about $20.00. Such unusual items as bud and flower vases, syrup dispensers, ashtrays, candle holders, marmalade containers, and covered casseroles were offered at extra cost. Fiesta red, it is said, "Went to War" in the 1940s along with cobalt blue and Lucky Strike green. A rumor, since dismissed, persisted that Fiesta red, the most expensive color in the line, was "radioactive." By the 1940s, softer colors such as rose, chartreuse, forest green, and gray were created for the Fiesta line.

During the 1930s millions enjoyed their coffee and doughnuts, America's most popular morning, afternoon, or evening snack, in Mother's breadline kitchen served on Depression glass or Fiesta ware. Always, steaming-hot black coffee was poured from a bubbling enamel percolator that Mother had purchased for 69¢ at the five-and-dime. In the breakfast nook or on the kitchen table covered with a flower-embroidered linen tablecloth you could savor coffee and munch delicious homemade doughnuts. Here is Mother's original Depression recipe for home-style doughnuts the way Dad and the kids loved them.

MOTHER'S DEPRESSION DOUGHNUTS

2 cups sifted flour	½ cup sugar
2 level teaspoons	1 tablespoon melted
baking powder	shortening
¾ teaspoon salt	1 beaten egg
½ teaspoon nutmeg	½ cup milk
½ teaspoon cinnamon	

Sift the flour 3 times with the baking powder, salt, and spices. Combine the sugar, melted shortening, beaten egg, add dry ingredients alternately with the milk. Turn out on a well-floured board and roll to a ½-inch thickness. Cut with a doughnut cutter and fry in deep hot fat until a golden brown. Sprinkle with powdered sugar. Serve with java.

Moderne chromium coffee percolator, patented 1922.

One-pound coffee tins from The Great Atlantic & Pacific Tea Company: *left*, 1930s; *right*, 1920s.

Cosmetic and Fashion Vanities

The August 1930 issue of *Fortune* magazine stated: "The beauty business has swept the country in the last decade with a speed and volume no less astounding than the radio, refrigerator or road-building industries."

Cosmetics in 1930 became a $2 billion business with advertising budgets rising higher than those for automobiles and food. This marketing process continued an upward trend, with many companies developing new merchandising methods and creating modern concepts in packaging and design. Many vivid Art Deco patterns are found on talcum-powder tins, rouge pots, compacts, and face-powder boxes of the 1920s and 1930s. Princess Pat, Tangee, Max Factor, and Outdoor Girl products were all offered at the five-and-dimes and drugstores in attractively designed containers. Tangee Lipstick, with its advertising slogan "Avoid that painted look," sold for 34¢ for the two-ounce size and 10¢ for the small trial size. The Princess Pat cake rouge introduced new bright red colors for dry rouge with names like Squaw Raspberry, Theatrical Strawberry, and Vivid Poppy.

Women began to adopt a new, modern image, aided by cosmetics and other vanity products, starting at their boudoir mirrors with the latest "miracle" cold creams that purportedly contained "precious oils." Prior to the mid-1920s only showgirls or actresses would exhibit themselves in public places wearing noticeable makeup. The artificial Egyptian and Chinese sculptured look was a Hollywood image that Garbo, Dietrich, Hepburn, and Crawford helped to sell to a beauty-starved public. Pencil-thin, highly arched brows, long false eyelashes blackened with thick mascara, intense blue or green eye shadow, bright red lips, a white powdered face and applied dry rouge created an almost masklike Dragon Lady appearance that many women tried to emulate. This became the modern Art Deco vamp style for women who wanted to appear to be as ultraglamorous and sophisticated as the stars. Jean Harlow had her influence on the fashion of the age when her mentor Howard Hughes ordered her hair to be bleached out to a pale white-blonde. Much was written about Jean Harlow's "platinum" hair, and women across America went to the corner drugstores to purchase a package of white henna bleaching compound, which they mixed with a bottle of 20-volume peroxide. Products such as Blondex Shampoo perpetuated the myth of a new, better life offered through lighter, shinier, and "blonder" hair. Betty Grable, Alice Faye, Toby Wing, and Lyda Roberti became known in Screenland as Hollywood "cosmetic" blondes. Modern beauty could be created through artifice, and American women were now eager to believe in and buy these new products.

Hairstyles in the 1920s were straight, bobbed or upswept; but by the 1930s hair had to be machine-waved into sculptured "marcelled" (so called after the French hairdresser Marcel Grateau who originated the marcel wave) dips close to the head in a pseudo-Grecian manner. Every 1930s housewife and working woman dashed to her local beauty parlor to have an "electric permanent," either in a molded contour style or fashioned after the tight crimp curls preferred by Ginger Rogers, Eleanor Powell, or Deanna Durbin. Some beauticians instructed customers never to comb their permanent waves out, and to cover their set with a hairnet. By the 1940s thick

Lady's compact: green and black enamel on silver, 1928.

Porcelain powder box, displaying seated flapper, for a vanity, Germany, 1926.

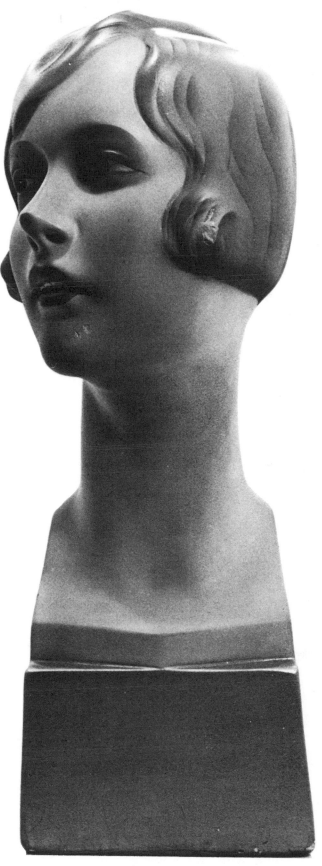

The look of the 1920s: airbrushed plaster, life-size mannequin head with short bobbed hair.

Decorative "Seventeen" face-powder box from Colgate, c. 1930.

hairnets or crocheted snoods became a fashion must so that defense plant workers could avoid getting their hair snarled in machinery. Paramount star Veronica Lake was asked by her studio to clip off her famous long blonde "peekaboo" bang to set an example for the war effort; her shorter, Claudette Colbert-style feathercut actually diminished her box-office appeal with movie fans.

In the 1920s, the flapper era, dresses, although short, had been loosely fitted with the waistline set well below the hips. The 1930s returned the waistline to the waist and featured lower hemlines that concealed the legs, and hips and bust lines again were emphasized. The modern image for women was a classic one with clothes streamlined to the body's natural contours. Pointed, thin, high-heeled shoes molded madam's feet into slender silhouettes. The cloche hats of the 1920s gave way in the 1930s to slouch headgear with wide brims or elaborate felt crowns, featuring dramatic veils, feathers, and artificial flowers. Adrian introduced the new fashion change for the 1940s—shoulder pads, skirts raised above the knee, thick-platform high-heeled shoes, and exaggerated, upswept hairdos incorporating "rolls" or "rats" to make women appear taller. This military, masculine, almost "clumpy" look

Caricature of a woman getting a permanent, *Judge* magazine, May 1929.

Blondex products for blondes. Complexion soap and box, c. 1928; shampoo box, c. 1937.

gave way to another style just after the end of World War II when Dior brought from Paris his New Look, which was to stay with us well into the 1950s: long, full skirts with layers of puffy-stiff crinoline slips underneath, which resembled the hoopskirts of the Civil War period—these worn with pancake-flat ballerina-slipper shoes. Frilly feminine blouses and softer pageboy-style hairdos, half bangs, and ponytails reinstated a more girlish, gamin effect following the harsh years of the war.

Men's fashions were fairly standardized in the 1920s and 1930s: the trim, svelte styling in clothes epitomized by the dapper look of Fred Astaire or Noel Coward: suits, shirts, ties, long, silk polka-dot dressing gowns, and slim, pointed, flat-heeled shoes. In the 1940s and 1950s fashion for men seemed to become more loose and blousy with almost no body contours except in military uniforms. Occasionally, men would be permitted a "novelty" item in clothing such as the bright red and green reindeer, Indian, or polar-bear sweaters from Jantzen or McGregor Sportswear, or loud, lotus-blossom Hawaiian shirts like those popularized by Harry Truman. Not until the psychedelic 1960s did men begin to acquire a more distinct and variable self-image.

Ciel Bleu powder box made by Cheramy, Paris, c. 1930.

Men's wool "Indian" sweater by Campus, Inc., c. 1943.

Fashion image of the 1930s: marcelled hair, penciled brows, dramatic half-turban hat, *Delineator* magazine, February 1934.

2.
LISTEN AND DREAM YOUR TROUBLES AWAY

The Radio Boom

Father sits in his favorite overstuffed easy chair reading about Hitler's latest triumph in Europe as Mother crochets a table doily under a dimly lit bridge lamp. Junior, his face covered with chocolate from a Mars' Milky Way bar, is caught up in Big Little Book adventures, with the family terrier, Jiggs, snoozing at his side. What do you do? You think of strolling to the corner candy store where you might drop a nickel into the brightly lit Wurlitzer, perhaps swoon over the latest melodies from Tommy Tucker's, Sammy Kaye's, or Glen Gray's orchestra and indulge in an ice-cream sundae. Instead, since heavy snow has begun to fall, you decide to stay indoors, switch on the family Zenith console, dig into a box of crackers and enter the suspenseful world of "I Love a Mystery." At some point Mother will insist you change the Magic Green Dial to "One Man's Family," "The Kate Smith Show," or "Fibber McGee and Molly." Such was the setting for a long winter's evening at home with an American middle-class Depression-World War II family.

Radio was the most all-encompassing, all-pervading, and all-powerful entity to invade the public consciousness in the 1930s. Although wide-scale manufacturing

Novelty microphone for use at home with a wireless set from Wonder Specialties Inc., Cleveland, Ohio, 1925.

Miniature crystal radio set in box from Philmore Mfg. Co., Inc., New York, c. 1927.

Sheet music inspired by the early wireless radio, 1922.

Early radio sheet music, 1921.

of radio sets began in 1920, it was not until 1927 that the "AC plug-ins" brought the wonder of this new medium into "everyday-permanent-household" status in American life. Early radios, the crystal sets, and the wireless with its complicated paraphernalia and separate cornucopia speakers, have roots going as far back as 1887 and continue in the experimental, novelty, and hobbyist phases up to the mid-1920s. In 1928 radios were popping out of the factories into salesrooms at the rate of about 75,000 per week. By 1929, and through the worst years of the Depression, 26 million people owned sets, representing eighty-five percent of the populace. In 1938 you could purchase a radio for $9.95, but the average cost was $50.00 for a six-tube model, and the product itself or "hardware" was greatly improved. The communications impact was tremendous, breaking down the barrier of regionalism and narrowing the gap between city and country folk. Even more than the movies, radio became the great synthesizer of middle-class sensibilities; and with the ether "burning nightly" through the airwaves and seeping into the living room, middle-class consciousness was raised to a new level of awareness through radio communication. Listening to the radio became a steady family routine, and, by the 1940s, there was at least one radio in every home and one in most cars.

With just the single dimension of sound, radio pulled the listener into new worlds of imagination. Thus the crude gadgetry of a sound man hitting coconut shells against a soundboard to create the hoofbeats of a horse—or crumpling cellophane near a microphone to produce the sound of fire—gave the radio audience a chance really to "participate" in this new imaginative auditory medium. The mass appeal of the radio set revolutionized communications for news, entertainment, and advertising. Going beyond newsprint, on-the-spot news coverage could be supplied around the clock; ball games, prizefights, and political races were brought right into the living room as they happened. An incident that created a great impact on audiences was reported in 1937 by radio announcer Herbert Morrison amid tears and in a choked trembling voice, heard against the background of a screaming, hysterical crowd. The *Hindenburg* zeppelin, arriving at Lakehurst, New Jersey, exploded in midair, and Morrison gave a searing, moment-to-moment live account of this to stunned radio listeners.

Frequency modulation (FM), although invented in 1933, didn't flourish until after World War II. The same was true of television, which had been available in 1938, but, due to early technical and economic problems, did not become a commercial possibility until 1946 when it had an impact similar to that of radio in the late 1920s.

R.C.A. Victor console radio in black-lacquer cabinet supported by a chromium-plated, tubular-steel framework, c. 1930.

Streamlined, dark-brown Bakelite, Zenith "Baby" radio, 1935.

Radio Sets

A console radio set was a big four-legged piece of furniture housing six to eight, or more large tubes, a speaker system, and often concealing the added feature of a 78 rpm phonograph inside the cabinetry. Squeaky battery-operated radio consoles were available in the early 1920s, but had little popularity until the AC plug-in sets created for use in any home electrical outlet made them a practical reality in 1927; and

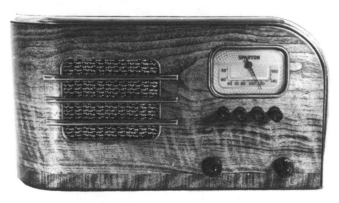

Sparton metal radio in "automotive style" with imitation wood grain made by Sparks-Withington Co., 1935.

Sparton radio in blue mirror on a black-lacquered base with chromium decoration, made by Sparks-Withington Co., 1933.

by 1929, the big consoles joined other prominent furniture in the living room and became its new focal point. A Stromberg-Carlson eight-tube console cost $380 in 1929 and an RCA Radiola sold for $575. Atwater Kent and Stromberg-Carlson were in the quality class, but the most popular sets were from Philco, Zenith, and RCA, the last with its trademark fox terrier listening to a trumpet speaker. Radio became less expensive as America went from the early stages of the Depression into the late 1930s when many Americans were buying them on the installment plan, $5.00 down and $5.00 monthly.

The cathedral-style radio was the first table model; but in 1932 the "baby" model, operating on either alternating or direct current made its appearance in the radio market. Prices for these portable 5-pound "babies," eight to ten inches long, six inches in height and four inches deep, were scaled from a low $7.50 up to $40.00 with Emerson Radio Corporation leading in this market. By 1933 baby radios accounted for sixty percent of all sales.

Radios improved technologically from the early to the late 1930s; and well-known industrial designers were hired to lead cabinets out of the Rosebud Gothic or Gingerbread lines into the sleeker contours of streamlined Moderne. The primary motivation was to spur sales by redesigning cabinets as often as deemed profitable. Designers were delighted to comply and complained that they could go a lot further with modernism if the public were not committed to middle-class ponderosity in its furniture taste. Many smaller sets produced by Emerson, Cyart, DeWald, and Fada were molded in bright yellow, orange, red, white, or green Catalin and are good examples of the "aerodynamic streamlined Moderne" styling, a rounded teardrop curve on one side with two angular corners on the other, resembling, in effect, the new automotive contours employed in the advanced de-

Pla-Pal Prohibition hidden-bar-and-stash radio in wood, chrome, and black enamel trim, 1925.

Pla-Pal with top and sides open.

signs of the Chrysler-De Soto Airflows (1935–1936), or appearing, at other times, to coincide with the new futuristic "Century of Progress" modern architecture. The Sparks-Withington Company, a forerunner in modernistic radio design, produced Sparton Radios, deliberately meant to resemble automobile dashboards, incorporating cobalt-blue or peach mirror with chromium-metal strips and black-enameled wood in striking Art Moderne cabinets. These better pieces were often found in penthouses or in the modern lounge of a hotel and were in demand with Hollywood movie stars. The Majestic Company sold novelty Charlie McCarthy radios that had a Charlie replica sitting elegantly on a ledge indentation as if overseeing the controls; and Emerson did well in the field with their early pop-art-style Mickey Mouse, Snow White, and Three Little Pigs radios, the housings made in Syroco, a pressed wood.

Radio Advertising

Radio advertisers spent $100 million in 1937; and one agency put forth the dictum: "a program must entertain, yes, but even the most entertaining program is a flop if it doesn't *sell merchandise*." Other than free "come-on" offers of booklets, knickknacks, or premiums, advertisements on radio had to sell hard and become identified with a "winner" program. The radio audience was a purchasing one that had advertising agencies competing fiercely for prime spots. The most popular types of products sold on radio in order of their sales importance were: drugs and toilet goods; foods and beverages such as coffee and soda; automobiles; tobacco products; laundry soaps and housekeeping supplies; petroleum products, lubricants and fuels; radios and phonographs; confectioneries like candy, gum, or ice cream; home furnishings, and kitchen equipment.

Broadcast Advertising, book published by National Broadcasting Company, 1929.

Sinclair road map featuring the Sinclair Minstrels jazz band, 1933.

Charlie McCarthy Majestic radio in white enamel on metal with the figurine in painted metal alloy, 1938.

The effects of radio advertising were astounding. Campbell's sold twice as much chicken soup at the food stores when first advertised on "Hollywood Hotel." When the Sinclair Refining Company announced on a radio broadcast that one million dinosaur poster stamps would be distributed free at local filling stations, they were grabbed up within forty-eight hours by one million kids. In 1930 the Ziegler Company, when introducing Betty Jane candy at the Midwestern station WTMV on a call-in song identification program, instigated the sale of twenty-seven tons of the sticky Betty Jane concoction in just five weeks. When Kate Smith first plugged A&P coffee, sales jumped twenty-five percent in one week. Radio advertisers and their industrial backers stood staunchly behind middle-class American morality in programming and marketing concepts, protecting these virtues at all costs. An impertinent announcer or comic who "slipped" could suddenly find himself shafted for an indiscretion—unless that person happened to be Arthur Godfrey or Fred Allen, both of whom had developed such a strong identification with the American public that their sarcastic comic assaults on a product could actually contribute to putting it over.

Programming

Radio periodicals selling at newsstands were *Radio Stars*, *Radio Guide*, *Radioland*, and *Popular Music*, most of which featured full weekly program listings, news tidbits about radio series and radio personalities, as well as feature articles on the medium itself. The two highest powered radio networks were NBC (the National Broadcasting Company with two networks; identified respectively as the Red and the Blue) and CBS (the Columbia Broadcasting System)

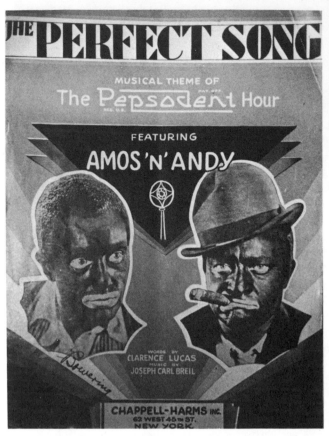

"Amos 'n' Andy" radio-theme sheet music, dated 1939.

Kate Smith's autobiography published by Blue Ribbon Books, 1938.

Kate Smith "God Bless America" electric clock made in Chicago, 1940.

Charlie McCarthy Scrap Book, Western Tablet Co., 1935.

Wrigley's Gum promotional calendar featuring radio's popular soap-opera stars, Myrt & Marge, 1934.

with key stations like WABC, WEAF, WJZ, and WOR presenting prime-time programs of note to millions of Americans: Orson Welles's "Mercury Theatre of the Air"; "Mr. First Nighter" with Les Tremayne; "Grand Central Station"; Phil Baker's "Take It or Leave It"; "The $64 Question and Answer Show"; "The Fitch Bandwagon," featuring Alice Faye and Phil Harris; "The Eddie Cantor Show"; "Henry Aldrich," starring Ezra Stone and Jackie Kelk; Fanny Brice as "Baby Snooks"; and "The Happiness Boys," Billy Jones and Ernie Hare, who claim the title to radio's first big humor show, which lasted from 1921 through 1939.

The top program in all radio history was "Amos 'n' Andy," two black characters from Harlem, played by two white former vaudevillians, Freeman Gosden and Charles Correll. Thirty million tuned in every weekday, Monday through Friday at 7:00 P.M., to this fifteen-minute show, which was on the air without interruption from 1928 to 1960. So popular were these radio rogues, who opened their show by yelling out "ow wah, ow wah, ow wah," that department stores that were open in the evening had the broadcast piped in for shoppers afraid to miss an episode, and movie theatres scheduled their features to end before seven so they, too, could offer the beloved Amos, Andy, Kingfish, Lightnin' and Henry Van Porter, all played by the same two actors, over their sound systems.

The second program in all-time high ratings was "Fibber McGee and Molly," portrayed by Marion and Jim Jordan, which was on the airwaves from 1931 to 1959 under the sponsorship of Johnson's Wax. Fibber's opening of the hall closet and the subsequent crash, followed by his exclamation, "gotta straighten out the closet one of these days," was a weekly event not to be missed in most households.

Hopalong Cassidy chrome-and-black-metal Arvin radio, dated 1950.

Another perennial favorite, "One Man's Family —dedicated to mothers and fathers of the younger generation and their bewildering offspring," was the longest running noninterrupted serial in the history of radio, remaining on the air from 1932 to 1959. Kate Smith, the highest-salaried female radio star, had one of the best of the music-variety shows with up to sixteen million avid fans listening to her dreamy theme-intro—"When the Moon Comes Over the Mountain"—each Thursday. "The Kate Smith Show," also known as the "A&P Bandwagon," opened with Kate's familiar and cheerful "Hello, everybody," and ended with a charming "thanks for listening, goodnight folks." The robust Miss Smith was once introduced by Franklin Roosevelt to the Queen of England with an emphatic "This *is* America!" So powerful was her legend among radio listeners that during World War II, with the singing of Irving Berlin's "God Bless America," she sold $600 million worth of War Bonds and raised $4 million for the Red Cross, leading President Truman to cite her for the Legion of Honor.

As live stage vaudeville disappeared, the radio industry was eager to hire the expertly trained unemployed comics, fast ad-libbers who were adept at improvising a new format each week. What the public wanted most, according to the industry itself, was plenty of comedy, a variety of singers, star guest shots, and live bands. "The Chase and Sanborn Hour," starring ventriloquist Edgar Bergen and his perspicacious dummy Charlie McCarthy, was this type of successful format show that invited weekly guests such as John Barrymore, W. C. Fields, and Tallulah Bankhead to converse with the witty and sardonic Charlie and his oafish sidekick Mortimer Snerd. "The Lux Radio Theatre," hosted by Cecil B. De Mille, was on the air from 1936 to 1955 with its "Lux . . . . presents Hollywood"; it offered adaptations of famous motion pictures and employed movie stars in leading dramatic roles. The very first program featured Marlene Dietrich and Clark Gable in "The Legionnaire and the Lady" adapted from the film *Morocco*. The second week it was Myrna Loy and William Powell in "The Thin Man"; and "The Lux Radio Theatre" went on to present such movie favorites as Barbara Stanwyck, Claudette Colbert, Loretta Young, and Fred MacMurray, week after week.

Daytime programming was geared to housewives who wept happily over the ironing board from 10:00 A.M. to 4:30 P.M. listening to fifteen-minute soap operas, usually sponsored by a soap product such as Oxydol, Chipso, or Duz. Marital difficulties, amnesia, chronic illness, alcoholism, disappearing persons—all backed up by simpering melodies like "Those En-

dearing Young Charms" pumped out on the organ— were the métier of the soaps, with "Mary Noble, Backstage Wife" as mother's special favorite. These serial melodramas tended to stress characterological nuance rather than plot, and it was to the characters, rather than the actors, that hordes of fan mail was sent. Other long-running soaps were "The Romance of Helen Trent," "Life Can Be Beautiful," "Stella Dallas," "Portia Faces Life," "John's Other Wife," "Our Gal Sunday," and "Ma Perkins" played by Virginia Payne, who doled out practical advice to distraught housewives for twenty-seven years. Another popular show, "Myrt and Marge," was sponsored by Wrigley's Chewing Gum. The actresses Myrtle Vail and Dora Dameral, who were idols to teenage girls, were mother and daughter in real life as well as in radio fiction. Special recipe advice programs such as "Aunt Sammy's Radio Recipes," "Betty Crocker," or "Aunt Jemima" asked mother to send in flour box tops for special home cookbook giveaways.

At 4:30 P.M. the soaps gave way to children's shows. The kids would rush home from school to listen to their favorite pre-supper radio fantasy pals, "Superman," "Mark Trail," "Dick Daring," "Hop Harrigan," "Sky King," "Flash Gordon," "Buck Rogers in the 25th Century," "Hopalong Cassidy," "Smilin'

Emerson Mickey Mouse radio, 1933. © Walt Disney Productions.

Jack," "Bobby Benson's Adventures," or the "Betty Boop Fables" starring Mae Questel as Betty.

Walt Disney originated the "Mickey Mouse Theatre of the Air," which was first heard in 1937 with Mr. Disney himself doing the high-pitched vocalizing for Mickey Mouse. Other characters featured in the Silly Symphony radio cast were Clara Cluck, Goofy, and Clarabelle Cow with a Donald Duck Swing Band featuring Minnie Mouse's Woodland Choir. Children's shows were a boon to advertisers who offered special radio premiums from a radio hero or heroine for a box top and, sometimes, an additional nickel or dime to kids who longed to be a part of the world of radio adventure.

Shows offering premiums were the most popular, and at the height of the Depression in 1933, the "Tom Mix" radio program hit the top of the list by sending out the greatest number of gift rings, toys, and badges. The first radio premium was a Tom Mix Horseshoe Nail Ring that you could obtain with a box top from Shredded Ralston, the breakfast food. "Boys! Girls! I'll send you my mystery ring *FREE!* for two Ralston box tops or one Ralston box top and 10¢ in coin." Cowboys Tom Mix, Gene Autry, Roy Rogers, and Hopalong Cassidy had a special place in the hearts of American youngsters yearning to explore the folklore and mysteries of the Wild West. The most mythical radio cowboy folk hero of this era was the Lone Ranger, who, riding his famed horse Silver to the strains of the Overture to *William Tell,* called out a hearty "Hi-yo Silver, Awa-ay!" to excited young listeners everywhere. Silvercup Bread, the Masked Rider's sponsor, gave away "silver bullet" ball-point pens and a cowboy belt, and the toy market was

flooded with holsters, guns, dart boards, and other Lone Ranger character items.

Quaker Oats brought the comic-strip detective Dick Tracy to the air, cajoling kids to send away for badges, an official comic-character watch, and a membership in Dick Tracy's Secret Service Patrol. Jack Armstrong, radio's All-American Boy, issued his own secret whistle rings, shooting disks, and other "crime-smashing" premiums to boys eager to keep America a clean and safe place in which to live. FBI man and self-styled pop-culture folk hero Melvin Purvis also got into this merchandising act. After ambushing and killing America's most dangerous Depression criminal, John Dillinger, he went on through a contract with Post Toasties to promote Junior G-Man Clubs foisting "authentic" FBI magnifying glasses, fingerprint sets, and G-Man kits upon dutiful crime-conscious junior Americans who enjoyed playing the game "cops and robbers." The radio show "Junior G-Men" was first heard over the Mutual network in 1936.

However, no merchandising effort was as successful or well known as Little Orphan Annie's radio association with the Wander Company, makers of Ovaltine, the pep-up chocolate energy drink. Taken from Harold Gray's *Chicago Tribune* comic strip, Orphan Annie was first heard over the Blue network with Shirley Bell as the voice of Annie in 1931. Orphan Annie, "the chatterbox with the pretty auburn locks," and her dog Sandy, barking "Arf" whenever his mistress was in trouble, were Depression favorites who gained full popularity with children and also won acceptance with the general radio audience. One Ovaltine label sent to the station could obtain for the listener an orange-top Ovaltine Beetleware Shake-Up mug with a colorful decal depicting Annie with Sandy, shaking the delicious chocolate energy

Official Gangbusters "Crusade Against Crime" toy machine gun, color lithograph on metal with wood, Louis Marx & Co., c. 1936.

Lone Ranger school lunch box, color lithograph on metal, 1948.

drink in their own microcosmic-size Orphan Annie mug into infinity, while the orphan-urchin cried out, "Leapin' lizards! For a real treat yuh can't beat a cold Ovaltine shake-up! It's good-tastin' an' good *for* yuh, too!" Membership in Orphan Annie's Secret Society entitled kids to game-board maps, Orphan Annie paper masks, rings, decoder badges, bracelets, and special Secret Society yearly booklets. Little Orphan Annie went off the air in 1942 and "Captain Midnight" took over her Ovaltine sponsor and offered World War II children a new Captain Midnight Ovaltine Shake-Up mug in bright vermilion with a blue top and other giveaways, including membership in the Captain's own Secret Squadron. Later, on TV, Ovaltine sponsored "Howdy Doody," producing yet another plastic Ovaltine mug and cup that featured the famous television puppet.

At suppertime the Depression family listened to the well-known news broadcasters H. V. Kaltenborn, Gabriel Heatter, Drew Pearson, and Lowell Thomas. "The Answer Man," another suppertime favorite, had Albert Mitchell answering questions on a multitude of subjects sent in by curious listeners, such as "What is Hitler's private telephone number?" Prime evening

Little Orphan Annie ceramic mug with underglaze decal, Ovaltine radio premium, The Wander Co., Chicago, c. 1934.

Little Orphan Annie game board, The Wander Co., Chicago, dated 1933.

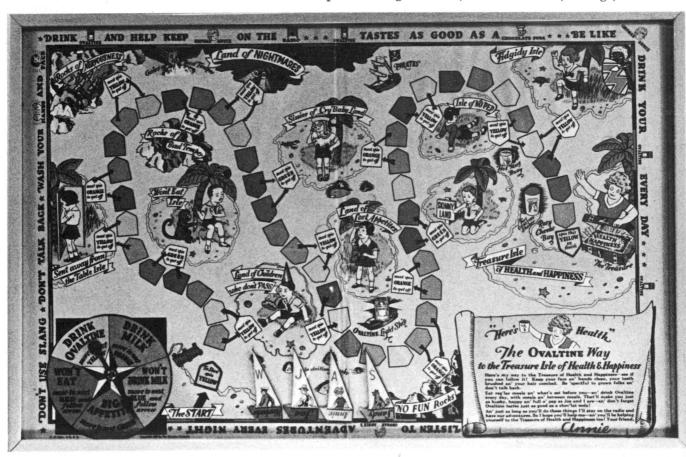

hours found the family gathered around the living room hardware and tuning in to a conglomeration of variety shows, amateur hours, comedians, dramas, mysteries, crime stopper shows, musical programs, and the "big bands." Specialty programs like Evangeline Adams doing her horoscopes, Robert Ripley's "Believe It or Not," or columnist Walter Winchell broadcasting his Hollywood or Broadway gossip were family favorites. Mystery and crime shows such as "Inner Sanctum" with its creaking door, "The Whistler," "Suspense," "I Love a Mystery," "Lights Out," "The Shadow," "Charlie Chan," "Bulldog Drummond," "The Falcon," "Mr. District Attorney," and "Gangbusters" kept the family on the edge of their seats. "Town Hall Tonight" (later known as "Allen's Alley"), with comedian Fred Allen and his wife Portland Hoffa, was aired on Sundays sponsored by Sal Hepatica, Ipana, and Minit-Rub. Other Sunday night big-time variety shows included Jack Benny, with his valet and best pal Rochester, sponsored by Jell-O, "The Burns and Allen Show" with the zany George and Gracie presented by Grape-Nuts Flakes, "The Rudy Vallee Show" introduced with Rudy's famous "Heigh-ho, everybody," and "The Hollywood Hotel" featuring Frances Langford and Dick Powell and movieland gossip columnist Louella Parsons. The world of radio held a special magic, and, it seemed, Americans could listen and dream away . . . forever.

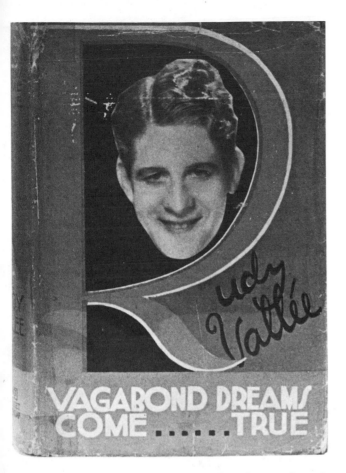

The autobiography of radio's "Vagabond Lover"—Rudy Vallee, published by Grosset & Dunlap, 1930.

Merchandising efforts of early TV stars Hopalong Cassidy and Howdy Doody, 1950s.

Music on the Air

The popular music heard in the late 1920s on early radio was predominantly Dixieland jazz and small hotel dance orchestras, with the big-band sound and swing coming to prominence in the 1930s. Favorite vocalists were "the original radio girl" Miss Vaughn DeLeath, radio's first crooner, who "crooned" softly to save tubes from wearing down; Jessica Dragonette; Ruth Etting; Frank Parker, star of the Rippling Rhythm Revue; Joseph White, the "Silver Masked Tenor"; "Smiling" Jack Smith—the singer with a "Smile in his Vocal Chords"; Gene Austin, "Radio's Whispering Tenor"; Bing Crosby; Alice Joy, Radio's "Dream Girl"; and Cliff Edwards, also called "Ukulele Ike." Singing sisters included the Frazee Sisters, Jane and Ruth; The Blossom Sisters, Helen and Dot; the Pickens Sisters, Jane, Helen, and Patty; The Lane Sisters, Priscilla and Rosemary; the Andrews Sisters, Patty, Maxine, and LaVerne; The Dinning Sisters, Lou, Jean, and Ginger; The DeMarco Sisters, Lilly, Mary, and Ann; and the Boswell Sisters, Martha, Connie, and Helvetia. Other groups were the Gold Dust Twins, Goldy and Dusty; The Smoothies, and the Tastyeast Jesters. Theme songs popularized on the radio were Rudy Vallee's "I'm Just a Vagabond Lover," Morton Downey's "Carolina Moon," Ben Bernie's "Au Revoir —Pleasant Dreams," Fred Waring's "Sleep," Glen Gray's "Smoke Rings," Bing Crosby's "Where the Blue of the Night Meets the Gold of the Day," and, of course, "When the Moon Comes Over the Mountain" as sung by Miss Kate Smith, "the Songbird of the South."

Orchestras that achieved prominence playing on the air were the Coon Sanders Nighthawks, Ben Bernie, Henry Busse, Benny Goodman, Glenn Miller, Ozzie Nelson, The Cliquot Club Eskimos, Richard Himber and his Ritz-Carlton Hotel Orchestra, Harry Horlick's A&P Gypsies, Bernie Cummins Hotel New Yorker Dance Orchestra, B. A. Rolfe, Kay Kayser with his Kollege of Musical Knowledge, Guy Lombardo, Russ Morgan, Ray Noble, Hal Kemp, Shep Fields, Lawrence Welk, Ted Weems, and Wayne King, "The Waltz King," featured on "The Lady Esther Serenade" radio show. Special feature orchestras like Fred Waring and his Glee Club or Phil Spitalny and his All-Girl Orchestra had developed vast followings among their radio audiences. Spitalny's "Hour of Charm" was hosted by Arlene Francis and featured the beautiful Evelyn and her Magic Violin.

Between 1934 and 1939, through the medium of radio as well as film, audiences were specifically developed who purchased phonograph machines, 78 rpm records, and sheet music featuring a radio star or a Hollywood musical film on its cover. Big, bubble-light jukeboxes with colorful lit-from-within yellow and red Bakelite side panels were put into restaurants, bars, and soda shops everywhere. By dropping a nickel into one of these mammoth machines, you could hear the latest hit platters from your favorite orchestras and vocalists. Sheet music was sold at five-and-dimes, specialty music shops, and at some department stores during the Depression. It was demonstrated by salesgirl-singers who accompanied themselves on the piano. Purchasing the sheet music and practicing it at home on the upright was a popular family pastime, its popularity in the 1920s diminishing somewhat in the 1930s due to the impact of radio. However, radio was not so much the culprit that caused this practice

to decline as the later hypnotic effect of television.

Macy's sheet-music department, the largest in New York City, listed these top-ten sellers for the month of January 1933:

1. All-American Girl
2. Let's Put Out the Lights and Go to Sleep
3. Play, Fiddle, Play
4. Say It Isn't So
5. How Deep Is the Ocean
6. Please
7. Fit as a Fiddle
8. We Just Couldn't Say Goodbye
9. Masquerade
10. A Shanty in Old Shanty Town

Sheet music from the 20th Century-Fox film *Wake Up and Live* starring Alice Faye—a radio-station comedy set in New York's Radio City, 1937.

Twelve-inch 78 rpm picture-record: "A Night with Paul Whiteman at the Biltmore," made by R.C.A. Victor Company, 1930.

3. THE TRANSPORTATION THEME

Automobiles

By the late 1920s accelerated growth in automobile production and in road building had opened up and changed the course of people's lives irrevocably. Americans had registered more than twenty-three million cars, and automobiles became the largest business in the country. Plant production of cars increased the demand in the steel, lead, paint, and rubber industries. In 1921, with the passing of the Federal Highway Act, the government entered into road construction. Pouring tar and cement over the old dirt horse-and-buggy roads brought about the additional necessity of upkeep which meant tighter controls, higher standards, and maintenance by state and federal governments. By the mid-1930s, the national highway system had developed 500,000 miles of two-lane roads with 375,000 miles fully paved. Families were less isolated and breadwinners commuted easily to distant jobs. Cities became decentralized as suburban developments mushroomed around them. A new fad—the family Sunday drive or picnic—put churches in a quandary over failing attendance—one of the "evils" created by the "lust" for automobiles. Nevertheless, by 1929, over sixty percent of auto sales were those made to families on the installment plan. Owning a car had become a definite social and economic status symbol, and often a young bachelor's success was judged by the quality or "make" of his machine.

The American public had had a love affair for many years with the old Model T Ford, but with the rapid changes occurring in society by 1926, it was branded "too cheap" and tagged "a jalopy" by competitors. The notion of speed had taken hold of the public, and drivers yearned to hit the open concrete roads behind high-compression engines that could push sixty miles per hour. Hopelessly attracted to four-wheel brakes, balloon tires, shock absorbers, a transmission and clutch, or any other new gadget that turned up on the market, buyers also wanted different body styles and colors other than the conventional black.

Auto production was a $1.5 billion business in 1930 but had diminished to $608 million by 1932 due

to "Old Man Depression." The "waterline" for pricing in the auto market of the early 1930s was $600. Below it, most manufacturers suffered, whereas above it one and a half million prospective customers could not afford to buy. Henry Ford, an early proponent of the assembly-line method of producing standardized component parts in volume, developed his new cheaper Model A in 1931, priced from $430 to $595 with 40 horsepower, 2,200 rpms, a conventional transmission, four-wheel mechanical brakes, and featuring a wide rear seat and big piston displacement. General Motors also came out in 1931 with a Chevrolet featuring six cylinders, 50 horsepower, 2,600 rpms, conventional transmission, four-wheel mechanical brakes, an air cleaner, and a valve-in-head motor at a price range of $475 to $634. In the same year Plymouth introduced a four-cylinder car that offered 56 horsepower, four-wheel hydraulic brakes, 2,800 rpms, and a special crankcase vent, an air cleaner, selective free-wheeling, intake silencer, and an automatic vacuum-spark control for $535 to $645.

Fortune magazine cover: truck transporting 1937 model cars, November 1936.

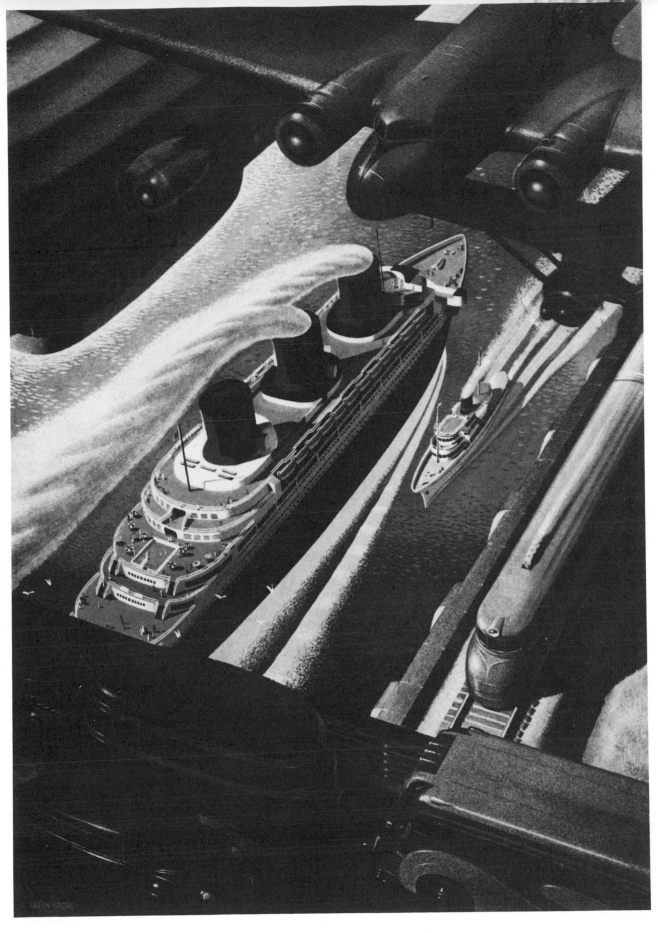

"Streamlined Transportation for Pleasure"—illustration from *Pleasure Magazine*, vol. 1, no. 1, Winter 1937.

DODGE

DE SOTO

HUDSON

CADILLAC

Sixteen 1938 cars that were previewed on October 27, 1937, at the National Automobile Show in New York. *Fortune* magazine, November 1937.

BUICK

GRAHAM

CHRYSLER

CHEVROLET

OLDSMOBILE

PONTIAC

HUPMOBILE

PACKARD

STUDEBAKER

NASH

PLYMOUTH

WILLYS

Streamlined modern design, sloped radiators and windshields, backswept fenders, and the torpedo shape began to appear in auto styling, notably in the Cord, Graham, Terraplane, Hupmobile, and Willys, all of which had futuristic body frames. The 1935 Auburn, which could perform at a speed of one hundred miles per hour, would also fit into this category although it was chiefly the Chrysler and De Soto Airflows that were the most influential and innovative producers of the new aerodynamic style, having had more effect on automotive design of the future than any of the other commercial models. The banner year for Detroit in terms of sales, design, and the introduction of revolutionary, new and modernistic features was 1935. Dealers sold 2,743,908 cars, and at the annual car show at Grand Central Palace in New York the public acquisitively examined fingertip gearshifts and syncromesh transmissions. In 1935, ninety-five percent of all cars sold in the United States cost less than $750. A 1936 Chevrolet coupe was $465, with Ford and Plymouth in the same price category. A Hudson-8 was $760, while the luxurious Cadillac V-16 was $3,500 without the extras. An average retail price

Car advertisement: a 1936 Dodge four-door sedan transports Shirley Temple to and from the studio.

Customized twin-6 Packard town car originally owned by Atwater Kent, the radio magnate, early 1920s.

for this year was about $580. The big three, Ford, General Motors, and Chrysler Corporation, led in sales, and the nation's favorites included Pontiac, Dodge, Chevrolet, Ford, Cadillac (V-8, V-12, and V-16), La Salle, Buick, Plymouth, De Soto, Nash, Chrysler, Oldsmobile, Lincoln, Hudson, Packard, and Studebaker.

The Studebaker Corporation suffered, with many other American business enterprises, in the Depression's worst year, 1933. With a lack of cash and with bankers demanding note payments, the company entered receivership. Rather than face bankruptcy, it launched a $100,000 advertising campaign and asked for a bond of loyalty from its dealers who called it "The Friendliest Auto Factory." Company committees convinced the creditors that Studebaker Corp.'s remaining in business would be to their own advantage. The public responded to this advertising blitz and Studebaker remained solvent. Many auto manufacturers in the Depression experienced similar mishaps, but, of course, not all recovered.

Packards were originally built in 1899 by a young magnate from Warren, Ohio, named James Ward Packard, one of 1,400 starters in the auto industry of whom no more than a dozen survived the financial hazards of the 1930s. The Packard, generally acknowledged as one of the finest cars ever produced in America, was called "The American Rolls-Royce." In the 1920s the aristocratic Packard with its haughty slogan, "Ask the man who owns one," usually sold for $3,000 and more. In 1928 Packard sold 50,000 cars, a peak year at that point, and in 1928 and 1929 it earned $25 million in the "class" market; but with the impact of the Depression, the company was forced to compete in the lower-priced markets of Pontiac and Buick. It responded with an eight-cylinder car for $1,000 and a six-cylinder car for $800, while continuing to produce luxury models including limousines and four-door convertibles. The company grew during the Depression and entered the post-World War II era but was finally forced out of the business in 1956. Ironically, by 1954 Packard had reached a

Custom super-8 formal Packard sedan originally owned by the five-and-dime millionaire, W. T. Grant, 1940. Owned by Al Trommer. Photograph by Tim Bissell.

pinnacle in automotive engineering. A fatal business merger with Studebaker and the full emergence of the era of the cheap disposable in America in the mid-1950s contributed to Packard's inability to maintain its high quality standards; and consequently the nation had to bid farewell to a great automotive heritage.

The most incredible car ever built in America was the Duesenberg, which arrived on the market December 1, 1928. This was a car for the wealthy connoisseur or for fabled film stars like Greta Garbo, whose S. J. model was recently sold at an antique car auction for $250,000. Produced by E. L. Cord, president of Auburn, and designed by Fred S. Duesenberg, this car was pleasant to drive, having superlative acceleration, speed, hill-climbing ability, and maximum reliability, offering its owners a superb machine with an exceptionally long life. The Duesenberg's main features were an eight-cylinder engine, 265 horsepower with 4.250 rpms, set in a chassis designed to handle this power with safety and optimum smoothness. The 1928 Duesenberg achieved 116 miles per hour in top gear at the Indianapolis Speedway and 89 miles per hour in second gear. The chassis then cost $8,500 with coachwork costing $2,500 more, and up.

World War II interrupted car production for civilian use but the postwar period brought another boom in the auto market. On June 28, 1945, the last of 8,685 bombers rolled from the huge Willow Run plant located just outside Detroit and Graham-Paige, the first new company to manufacture an American car in more than twenty years, moved in. In January 1946 it unveiled the startling new Kaisers and Frazers at the Waldorf-Astoria to throngs of onlookers who gazed in awe at the car that "symbolized the new look after the war." By April 15, 1946, the company had received 266,840 bona fide orders for the new 1947 Frazer.

Cars in the late 1940s and early 1950s were able to fulfill the ideal of the "American dream car" that was only a General Motors Futurama idea at the New York World's Fair of 1939–1940. The futuristic, rounded, squat scarab stylings of the Packard, Hudson, Lincoln, and Mercury of this period were an outstanding realization in automotive design and craft. The Studebaker, Cadillac, and Oldsmobile with their innovative use of heavy and ornate chrome, fin-shapes, bullet-face grilles and blue-tinted windshields transformed the American obsession with rocket ships and flying saucers into a new exaggerated fantasy mode for automobiles, but by the end of the 1950s, with the

1954 two-tone green, straight-8 Packard Patrician touring sedan, currently owned by the authors and featured in the film *Godfather II*. Photograph by Tim Bissell.

demise of the Packard and the Hudson, the dream of the superior American car faded away. The use of cheaper materials and the new industrial concept of planned obsolescence stultified the original thrust of automotive engineers and designers, and it is clear that Americans have settled back into a state of bland

complacency as far as automobiles are concerned. This may be one reason why more and more investigative minds are turning to the roots of early modernity for answers, as if the blueprint for progress had been lost somewhere in the past.

Showroom brochure introducing the 1947 Frazer.

Road maps from the 1920s, 1930s, and 1940s.

General Motors bronze ashtray from their Futurama at the 1939 New York World's Fair.

Gas Station Maintenance

During the Depression many families held onto the first car they purchased, extending its life ten years or more—not a difficult feat to begin with since most models were then built for longevity; and added to this, most men had to develop all kinds of mechanical skills in order to save money for the family's Depression budget. Those who could not play Mister Fixit used auto repair shops and gasoline stations, which doubled in number in the 1930s. Home auto maintenance also meant the development of new products and more advertising for this new, burgeoning market. Free road maps were offered to drivers, and the familiar Sunoco, Gulf, Tydol, and Shell gas stations, their brightly lit gas-pump globes designed to pull customers off the road, sold their gas for twenty-five cents or less per gallon. Service stations and specialty stores created many giveaways, including ashtrays, calendars, matches, and dolls, for promotional purposes and also advertised heavily on radio and television. Famous gasoline company logos such as the Texaco Star, Mobil's Flying Red Horse, Tydol's Flying "A," and the Sunoco "Sun" image became firmly imprinted in the car owner's mind. Chain stores like the Pep Boys, Star Auto, or the Eveready Company, famous for flashlight batteries, marketed their own popgraphic containers of antifreeze, oil, and radiator cleaners, as well as supplying car-happy Americans with a multitudinous array of tires, auto gadgetry, and other car extras and necessities.

Trains

Improved roads cut into train travel in the 1930s; and with more people buying and driving cars, it was inevitable that new concepts in railroading had to be developed. In 1934, under the leadership of designer Otto Kuhler, Pullman Incorporated built the first high-speed streamliner for public use. Named City of Salina, it was a lightweight, egg-shaped train enameled in brown and sunburst yellow. Union Pacific Railroad called it "Tomorrow's Train for Today." With a 600-horsepower engine, travel speeds of 110 miles per hour, a steel and chrome Moderne-style interior, and "air conditioning," it traveled from Omaha, Nebraska, to Washington, D.C., to be inspected by Franklin D. Roosevelt. Continuing a nationally advertised promotional tour through twenty-two states and making a great many show-stops, it wound up at the "Century of Progress" fair (1933–1934) in Chicago, where it was viewed by two million people. After making $700,000 in revenues and with 900,000 miles logged to its credit, this remarkable achievement in railroad design was scrapped for war materials in 1942. The Burlington Zephyr, a winner in design competitions, was the first to introduce a splendidly executed, gleaming stainless-steel exterior. Built by the Budd Manufacturing Company, the Zephyr was also exhibited at the Chicago world's fair in 1934.

Inspired by Roosevelt's New Deal, railroad magnates readily went into the building of modernized, air-conditioned streamliners. These new luxury trains

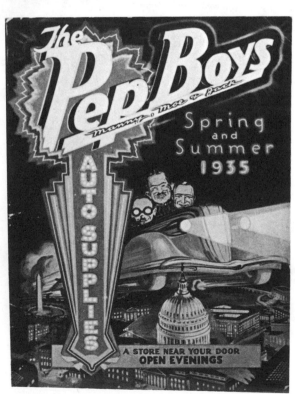

The Pep Boys catalogue of auto supplies and gadgets, 1935.

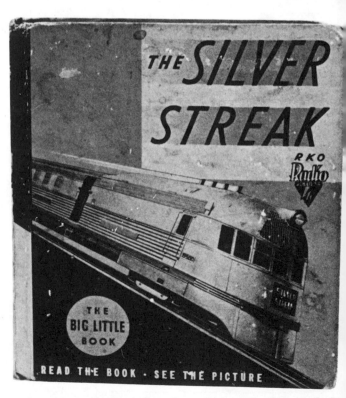

The Big Little Book based on the movie that used the Burlington Zephyr train as "The Silver Streak," 1935.

offered glamour and armchair comfort, stylish private compartments, Art Moderne cocktail lounges, and elegant dining cars. Advertisements stressed status—the "right" people, including movie stars, now traveled across America by rail. Trains noted for their contributions to modern design and engineering were the Blue Comet, the Super Chief, The 20th Century Limited, The Hiawatha, The Broadway Limited, the Silver Meteor, The Electroliner, and The Sunset Limited, all of which helped to fulfill Norman Bel Geddes's prediction that better designed, sleeker trains would inspire more travel by rail. Railroads reached the peak of excellence and commercialism between 1937 and 1939, but the cost of modernization—into the hundreds of millions—did not ultimately yield the anticipated profits. There was a resurgence of rail travel during the later war years, but after that period passenger interest dwindled and sumptuous streamlined trains gradually lost their attractiveness.

Planes

The first great men of aviation may have been the Wright brothers; but Charles Lindbergh with his famous solo flight across the Atlantic in 1927 in the single-engine plane *The Spirit of St. Louis* became America's national hero of air flight. In 1928 Rear Admiral Richard E. Byrd made his historic first flight over the South Pole, and in 1932 Amelia Earhart, the first woman to fly across the Atlantic alone, also became a heroine in the new field of modern aviation. Flyers continued to be worldwide idols in the Depression period. The whirring engine of a small, lightweight airplane above a downtown shopping area would often stop traffic as crowds gazed upward with wonder and admiration. Man's newfound ability to conquer the skies enticed the public. New speed and endurance records hit the headlines but so did the frequent mishaps.

Mail and passenger airplanes were in use in 1928 but were generally unsafe, with many crashes occurring; yet the feeling persisted that progress had to be served. Sky "daredevils" took to the air, defying the law of gravity in spectacular air circuses featuring stunt pilots who engaged in wing walking, complicated parachute jumps, barnstorming, and other

Nickel sculpture of a twin-engine plane mounted on a bronze lightning bolt, chrome ball, brass square, and marble base, c. 1938.

"Hello Lindy" sheet music, 1927.

daring feats. Amphibian planes, called flying boats, opened up remote areas for adventurous Americans. The China Clipper began service in 1936, providing luxury air travel between San Francisco and Hawaii, a 2,400-mile hop, and flying onward to the mysterious Far East. The most successful commercial airliner did not appear until 1937—the twin-engine DC-3, used extensively for many civilian purposes and eventually for military transport during World War II. By 1940 air travel was steadily on the rise, having doubled its passenger service since 1930.

Airships

The dirigible and the zeppelin were spectacles of majestic beauty as they floated serenely through and beyond the clouds. These huge silver bullet-shaped rigid airships became the vehicles for a novel and exciting type of air travel in the 1920s. Unfortunately, commercial air travel by dirigible ended in a series of disasters. The U.S.S. *Akron* plunged into the sea off Barnegat Light, New Jersey, in 1933 during an electrical storm, killing seventy-four people. Her sister ship, the lighter-than-air *Macon*, went down in February 1935 off Point Sur, California.

The *Graf Zeppelin* LZ 126, a long sleek passenger ship launched in 1928, was the predecessor to the most renowned commercial ship of all—the doomed German *Hindenburg*. Only a few feet shorter than the *Queen Mary*, the *Hindenburg* contained every luxury (including a dance floor) and for $720 for the round trip—between Germany and the United States—passengers experienced an incredible journey at a hitherto

The Story of the Airship, published by the Goodyear Tire & Rubber Co., 1925.

"Zep" canned cherries label, c. 1935.

unmatched airship-cruising speed of eighty-five miles per hour. Its maiden flight was in March 1936, but due to the fact that the United States refused to sell Germany helium, flammable hydrogen was used; and on May 6, 1937, after its third transatlantic crossing, the *Hindenburg* exploded while trying to dock at Lakehurst, New Jersey, with thirty-six passengers perishing in flames. This well-publicized disaster caused great public outcry, ending the short period of airship travel and permanently grounding the *Graf Zeppelin* and the other airships that were then in use.

Luxury Liners

If you could afford a "thrifty" vacation in 1933, you could purchase from the Dollar Steamship Company a boat ticket for $750 for an eighty-five-day cruise around the world. Some people enjoyed this kind of tour; but passengers traveling by ship were mainly in search of the luxury big ocean liners had to offer. Featuring lavish Art Deco and Art Moderne interiors created by the top designers and craftsmen of the day, these huge floating hotels contained churches, movie theatres, deluxe staterooms, pet kennels, smoker bars, full nightclubs, and mammoth public dining rooms. Among the most renowned and elegant of these big ships that will be remembered forever as the most glamorous and sophisticated mode of ocean travel were the *Normandie*, *L'Atlantique*, the *Ile de France*, the *Olympic*, the *Majestic*, the *Bremen*, and the *Queen Mary*.

Tri-motor "Boycraft" toy metal plane, 1930s.

Sinclair toy truck painted green, c. 1934.

Boys' Toys

Toy airplanes, trains, blimps, cars, and fantastic rocketships were best sellers in the department stores and five-and-dimes. Every young boy waiting to grow up needed such models in order to act out his secret fantasy thrills and danger-adventure games that were part of the everyday, real world of actual aviators, racers, or firemen. G-men, cops, and gangsters all maneuvered themselves about in cars, which always played an integral part in the dramatic action in gangster films, radio shows, and also in "real" FBI criminal chases. These toys provided vicarious experiences for the action-minded boy who, once grown up to manhood, longed for even greater velocity, entertaining even more bizarre fantasies fashioned around a "new modern world governed by machinery in motion." Adult periodicals of the era such as *Science and Mechanics*, *Science and Invention*, *Motor News*, or *Modern Mechanix* entranced many a would-be hobbyist or amateur inventor.

Most boys had to be content with smaller types of toy cars purchased from Woolworth's by a favorite aunt who presented them at Christmas or on birthdays. But what a variety of these were to be found in the Depression period! Toy cars were molded in melted lead, pot metal, cast iron, or rubber and were spray-painted on the assembly line just like "real" automobiles. The Dowst Brothers, leaders in the die-cast market, created the famous Tootsie Toy cars and also made tiny charms and miniatures for Cracker Jacks. Also in this toy car market were Barclay Mfg. Co., Man-Oil Co., The Kansas Toy and Novelty Com-

Bon Voyage card with ocean liner, clouds, and wave motif in Moderne style, 1935.

pany, the English import Dinky Toys, and Wyandotte, Inc., all of whom made cars, tractors, fire engines, tanks, and artillery trucks. The Louis Marx & Co., Courtland Toy Cars, and the German Schuco Co. made metal toys adding color lithography to the manufacturing process. The Sun-Rubber Company and Auburn-Rubber Company produced sturdy "imperishable" cars modeled after well-known brand autos such as Pontiac and De Soto. Oversize big metal pieces were manufactured by Buddy L. Trucks, Sonny, or Sturi Toys, while the Turnur Co. or Cor-cor turned out excellent heavy replicas of Packard cars, trucks, or buses. Well-known companies for cast-iron toys were Hubley, Arcade, Dent, Williams, and Kilgore, the last named also producing dollhouse furniture for the girls.

The Keystone Company and Boycraft created outstanding heavily constructed Ford tri-motor toy planes. Playing with one of these big, solid models permitted Junior to think of himself as an "aviation hero," later inspiring him to investigate books like *The Boy's Story of Lindbergh* or *Don Sturdy Across the North Pole*, literature that sent him further into "imagined flights of air conquest." Electric toy-train sets, replicas of actual Pullman and streamliner models, were special favorites at Christmastime under the tree, when Father and Junior would erect an entire miniature town with a station, painted-lead townspeople, stores, ice ponds made from blue mirrors, Log Cabin houses, and even a hollowed mountain range through which the toy train could speed, sounding an authentic whistle controlled by Junior from the transformer. The Lionel Corporation in three large factories in Irvington, New Jersey, produced three-fourths of the nation's toy electric trains with the biggest, shiniest toy locomotives and the widest assortment of cars.

Composed of metal and other sturdy "indestructible" materials, many of these handsome, first-rate toy cars, trucks, tanks, planes, and trains, created with one eye toward longevity and permanence, were turned over to government "scrap drives" during World War II; and the toy market has never again seen such fine machine-crafted and artful playthings.

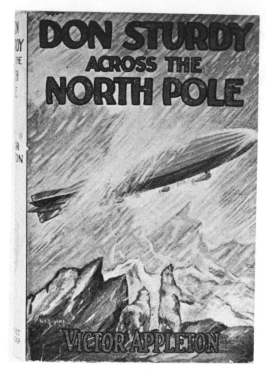

Don Sturdy Across the North Pole, with a dust jacket featuring a zeppelin, published by Grosset & Dunlap, 1925.

Child's metal pedal car, 1933.

Courtland windup mechanical car set, shown with original box, 1930s.

4. MICKEY MOUSE AND HIS FRIENDS AT THE FIVE-AND-DIME

The first Mickey Mouse toy: a wood-jointed doll featuring movable hands, arms, legs, feet, a painted composition head, and cloth-covered wire tail, produced in 1930 by George Borgfeldt Co. of New York. © Walt Disney Productions. Photograph by Tim Bissell.

A Mouse Is Born

The leading comic folk-culture hero to pop up out of a Depression-weary America was a bright, impish cartoon character called Mickey Mouse. A child visiting Woolworth's or Macy's toy department, or attending a Saturday movie matinee in the 1930s could not escape the impact of this cheery, indomitable creature conceived by Walter Elias Disney. Mickey appeared everywhere, and his image evoked instant glee from children and adults.

Many eminent artists and cartoonists today consider the early 1930s vintage Mickey Mouse to be the most perfectly developed abstract cartoon representation ever created. Rodentlike features, a white face, two black ovals with a wedge-shaped indentation for eyes, an exaggerated long nose ending in a black stub, rounded black balloon ears, a heart-shaped red tongue, a lengthy skinny black tail, stovepipe thin legs and arms, with short red pants held up by two large buttons, a pair of bulbous, clown-size shoes, and thick four-fingered gloves: this was certainly a combination that left an indelible imprint on the twentieth century.

Fortune magazine reported in November 1934:

> *Mickey Mouse is an international hero, better known than Roosevelt or Hitler, a part of the folklore of the world. It takes more than humor to achieve such renown. It takes quality, real and simple enough to cut deep into the emotions of people everywhere; and that quality, in whatever form you find it, is art.*

The idea for this happy mouse had its roots in and was influenced by both Charlie Chaplin's Tramp and Mickey's predecessor, Felix the Cat, created by Otto Messmer. Felix first appeared, looking doglike, in *Feline Follies* (1919), a silent cartoon; but he evolved in the mid- to late 1920s to become fuller in form and more catlike. Twenty-six Felix cartoons were produced annually through 1930, which pinpoints the end for Felix specifically as a cartoon star. Afterward he continued as a Sunday comic-strip character through

Photograph taken in 1927 of giant inflated "Felix the Cat" balloon float made for Macy's Thanksgiving Day Parade, shown in the Hoboken warehouse.

The Big Little Book based on the pre–Mickey Mouse Disney character, Oswald the Lucky Rabbit, from the Universal cartoon series, 1934.

Mickey Mouse Story Book, published by David McKay Co., 1931. © Walt Disney Productions.

1951, gaining popularity in the toy and doll market, although he was superseded in most areas by the ebullient Mickey. Oddly enough, a survey of children conducted in the 1930s revealed that half of those tots interviewed thought that Mickey Mouse was "a cat."

Mickey Mouse, Book 1, the first of the very early Disney books to achieve large sales, presented Mickey in "mouse-fiction" to millions of delighted readers. Published in 1931 by the David McKay Company, this book portrayed Mickey as a barnyard rodent who lived "in a cozy nest under the floor of the old barn" while his girl friend Minnie, in a polka-dot skirt, flower hat, and oversize pointy shoes, had a home safely hidden somewhere behind a chicken coop. A large ferocious cat named Claws would sit for hours staring at the hole-in-the-wall entrance to Mickey's home, where he had set up baited traps with cheese. Naturally it was Claws's own paw that got caught in the trap, to the squealing delight of Mickey and Minnie. Other comic characters introduced in this original barnyard tale were Clara Cluck, the operatic hen, and an extra-long-billed, squat Donald Duck. There was also an introduction in the form of a poem to the Silly Symphony, which had Mickey playing the drums, the fiddle, the bassoon, the xylophone, the horn, and the saxophone, while Minnie pounded away on the ivories.

The story of Mickey Mouse and his creator Walt Disney has by now become an integral part of American culture. Walt himself, born December 5, 1901, into a family of poor farmers, spent his first eight years among the farm and wild animals he would revere all of his life. As a boy he learned to do cartoon renderings of these animal friends, selling his pen-and-ink drawings, mostly of horses and pigs, to farm journals. Later, in young manhood, he became interested in the technique of animation, creating short cartoons that were shown at a small movie house in Kansas City. Encouraged by the response of the movie audience, Disney soon took out his first newspaper ad seeking professional employment as a maker of advertising cartoons and animated films. In 1919 he met Ub Iwerks, another enthusiastic comic artist, with whom he formed a company, capitalized at $15,000, called Laugh-o-Grams to produce cartoon shorts; but by 1923 they discovered they were heading into bankruptcy. Following this short-lived, somewhat disappointing venture, Disney went to Hollywood where he began developing *Alice in Cartoonland* shorts, featuring a real child acting along with the cartoon characters. Disney's brother Roy joined him there as business manager for this new series, and along with a staff of artists, including Iwerks, they turned out one "Alice" film every month over a period of several years, producing fifty-six of these live-action silent cartoons in all. In 1927 Disney developed a new cartoon character named Oswald, the Lucky Rabbit, who began to make regular appearances in a silent series distributed by Universal Pictures. After twenty-six of these "Oswald" cartoons had gained wide acceptance with the public, Disney embarked for New York to renegotiate a better financial deal; but, astoundingly, was offered a substantial reduction by the distributors. He then discovered that, due to a miniclause in his contract, he actually did not own the rights to his "lucky" rabbit, and this ended his connection with Oswald, who was later sold by Universal to Walter Lantz.

Embittered by what Disney felt to be an unfair and manipulative business tactic, he and his wife Lillian boarded a train back to Hollywood, California. En route, as legend has it, he remembered fondly a tiny friendly mouse that would come to visit him on his drawing board in earlier days, and he decided he would create a new comic character called Mortimer Mouse. Mrs. Disney thought Mortimer a much too high-class and grandiose name for a diminutive mouse and christened him Mickey instead.

In April 1928, Walt Disney with Ub Iwerks, his partner in the *Cartoonland* series, a new staff of artists, and his brother Roy, immediately began work on the first Mickey Mouse cartoon, *Plane Crazy. Plane Crazy* meant to parallel the nation's current obsession with air flight, and even Mickey himself sported a shaggy hairstyle like Charles Lindbergh's. Ub Iwerks completely illustrated and animated this first Mickey film; and many people continue to credit Iwerks for having created "the look" of the early mouse, although certainly Disney was always there in a leading role, writing scripts and shaping the personality of his beloved creation. *Gallopin' Gaucho* was the next Mickey cartoon; but before either was released, Disney went to see the first widely discussed "talkie," *The Jazz Singer* (1927), which starred Al Jolson in black-face pouring his heart out singing "My Mammy" to an enthralled movie audience. After seeing and hearing this film, Disney made the decision to add music and voices to his third Mickey cartoon. *Steamboat Willie* was the first talking cartoon, opening on November 18, 1928, at the Colony Theatre in New York; and it was a resounding success. Two weeks after its formal opening, it moved to the prestigious, and larger, Roxy Theatre, where audiences stood in line to hear a squeaky mouse speaking in Disney's own falsetto. *Plane Crazy* and *Gallopin' Gaucho* were subsequently released with sound added; and Mickey Mouse became firmly established as America's "first

Donald Duck molded soap figurine with box made by the Lightfoot Schultz Co., New York, 1938. © Walt Disney Productions.

"Mickey the Fireman," a homemade plaque jigsawed from wood and based on a hobby-magazine shop pattern, c. 1933. © Walt Disney Productions.

Three Little Pigs, book published by Blue Ribbon Books, 1933. © Walt Disney Productions.

Child's leatherette "Snow White and the Seven Dwarfs" purse, 1938. © Walt Disney Productions.

talking celluloid comic-character superstar," whose success enabled his creator to build a new animation studio and to reinvest in more and more Mickey cartoons.

Mickey films were turned out on a basis of one a month in the early 1930s, and the studio also began to diversify by creating "rhythmic cartoons" called Silly Symphonies. The first, released in July 1929, was called *The Skeleton Dance.* Film titles were always preceded by the legend "Mickey Mouse Presents a Silly Symphony"; and the first color Symphony cartoon was *Flowers and Trees,* a pastoral epic that opened at Grauman's Chinese Theater on July 30, 1932, earning Disney an Academy Award for that year as well as a special Academy Award for the creation of Mickey Mouse.

The first Mickey short in color was *The Band Concert* (1935), one of Disney's best, in which a blend of the Overture to *William Tell* with "Turkey in the Straw" and a quacking, obstreperous Donald Duck combined to create hilarious yet grotesquely beautiful moving images. The first onscreen appearance of the Duck had been in *The Wise Little Hen* (1934). In Mickey, Disney created a genuine American-style idol that was positivistic, earnest, and forthright in thought and action; but another leading character was needed that could express more specifically

the cathartic anger that was called for by a Depression public. These attributes were assigned to Donald Duck who gained fame by twirling and twisting his feathery torso in an agitated series of screaming "quacks" that endeared him to audiences as a close second to his happy pal, Mickey. Movie crowds projected whatever feelings they chose onto the Mickey Mouse image, according him the reverence usually expressed only for bona fide heroes or saints; but it was through Donald that they could realize their own emotions and frustrations often expressed by Donald in anger or open hostility. Mickey and Donald thus became perfect foils for each other.

Nineteen thirty-two was an auspicious year for Walt Disney, for he also produced one of his most memorable color Silly Symphonies, *The Three Little Pigs,* a longer cartoon that grossed $150,000 at the Roxy, where it was shown in three separate bookings the year it opened. Other than earning Disney yet another Oscar, the merry yet fearful Three Little Pigs and a leering, hungry Big Bad Wolf became popular symbols for the plight of America in the midst of the Depression. R. D. Feild in his book *The Art of Walt Disney* says of this period:

No one will ever know to what extent The Three Little Pigs *may be held responsible for pulling us out of the Depression, but certainly the lyrical jeer at the*

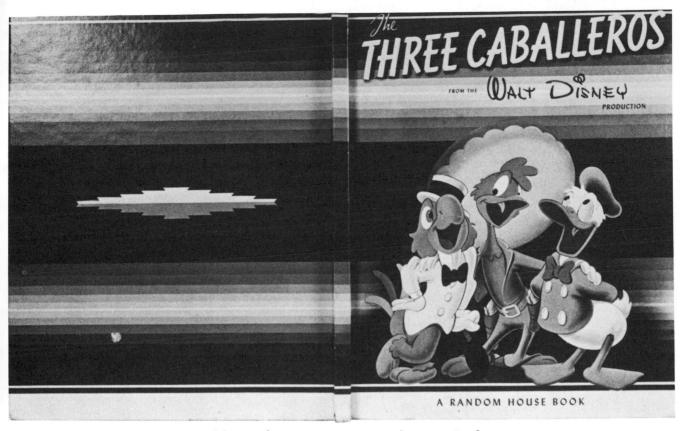

The Three Caballeros, book published by Random House, 1944. © Walt Disney Productions.

Big Bad Wolf contributed not a little to the raising of people's spirits and to their defiance of circumstance.

The Silly Symphonies aspired to art, which bestowed dignity on the animated cartoon for the first time, with support coming from both the critics and the public. Silly Symphony masterpieces such as *King Neptune* and *Babes in the Woods* were kept in a separate category from other first-rate cartoons like *Mother Goose Goes Hollywood* (1938), which caricatured such famous personalities as Greta Garbo, Mae West, and Charlie Chaplin, and notably *Ferdinand the Bull, Elmer the Elephant, Little Hiawatha, Tortoise and the Hare, Tugboat Mickey,* and *Santa's Workshop,* a film that Disney himself considered to be technically superior to *The Three Little Pigs.*

Disney's gigantic gamble in the 1930s was the creation of the first feature-length color cartoon *Snow White and the Seven Dwarfs,* which took four years to produce at the then formidable cost of $1.7 million. When it premiered in 1938 at New York's Radio City Music Hall, it gained instant recognition as a milestone in film history. It ran for five weeks at the Music Hall and grossed $8 million in its initial release. *Snow White* was subsequently shown in forty-one countries and its sound track was translated into ten languages. Snow White and her Seven Dwarfs became comic characters that followed Mickey Mouse and Donald

Duck into Disney's special Cartoon Hall of Fame.

Other major Disney animated features after *Snow White* were *Pinocchio,* premiering February 7, 1940; *Fantasia* (November 13, 1940); *The Reluctant Dragon* (1941), *Dumbo* (1941); *Bambi* (1942); *The Three Caballeros* (1945), which featured Donald Duck with Aurora Miranda, Carmen's sister, in live-action dancing with a new character, José Carioca, the sardonic South American parrot, *Song of the South* (1946), which had the Uncle Remus stories with live-action coupled with animation; *Fun and Fancy Free* (1947), which featured Edgar Bergen and Charlie McCarthy, Dinah Shore, and the Dinning Sisters; *Melody Time* (1948); *Cinderella* (1950), a big success that grossed $4 million in its first release; and *Alice in Wonderland* (1951).

Mickey retained his position as top Mouse, but as America entered the early years of World War II, he appeared to go through a metamorphosis from the familiar white-faced imp with a long tail into a rounder, pink, humanized appearance, becoming by the late 1940s even more anthropomorphic, looking at one point like a natty middle-aged Frank Sinatra mouse fully dressed in a zoot suit and minus a tail. This may be one reason Donald Duck gained in popularity during the war years; also, Donald could spit venom readily at a bully named Adolf Hitler whereas

Mickey often retained a more aloof attitude. Today a steady movement exists among fans to resurrect the early Mickey, with rodent features, white face, tail, red shorts, and squeaking mouseness intact.

During the 1940s both Donald and Mickey were employed by Uncle Sam in his go-to-war effort. At that time Disney historian R. D. Feild stated: "It may safely be said that Mickey has donned the uniform for the duration." Designed to help sell war bonds, Disney produced, in 1943, the films *Saludos Amigos,* which reflected a friendly South American good-neighbor policy, and *Victory Through Air* *Power,* the subject of which is strategic long-range bombing. Winston Churchill, who saw an early screening of the latter film, recommended it to Roosevelt, feeling that it might help the two allies in planning their war strategies. Another war cartoon, Academy Award-winner *Der Fuehrer's Face,* featured Donald Duck battling it out furiously with a caricatured Hitler and Mussolini.

Other than commercial films made for war purposes, Disney also developed specific training and morale-building films for the armed services. Beginning in 1942, Mickey, Donald, Goofy, and the other cartoon

"Der Fuehrer's Face," sheet music from a Disney short feature made during World War II, 1942. © Walt Disney Productions.

familiars were emblazoned on over 2,000 armed forces emblems and insignia made without charge to the government. Even Mickey's dog Pluto, the Seven Dwarfs, and the Three Little Pigs developed angry "fighting faces" for the march to war. Mickey images appeared on posters, bullets, bombs, hospitals, airplanes, and even the enemy painted him on some of their lethal weapons. D-i-s-n-e-y spelled A-m-e-r-i-c-a so emphatically for the Yanks and their allies that the secret password for the D-day landing became M-i-c-k-e-y-M-o-u-s-e. Many comic heroes "went to war": among them were Terry who fought the Japa-nese instead of pirates, Orphan Annie who got her Junior Commandos to collect scrap metal needed for the war effort, and Annie's own Daddy Warbucks, the former munitions-factory owner at the time of World War I who became "General" Warbucks in World War II.

After World War II, television sets entered the American living room and Mickey Mouse made a civilian comeback on the popular Disneyland Show in 1954. Following that, Walt launched his daily television show, "The Mickey Mouse Club," which featured the famed original Mouseketeers in a variety

"A March for Mickey Mouse" sheet music, 1934. © Walt Disney Productions.

format that brought kids cartoons, special lessons in dancing, singing, and school etiquette. The successful concept of Mickey Mouse clubs originated in 1929 as Saturday movie matinee organizations created to develop the patronage of youngsters, helping them to learn to become good citizens, to have good manners, and to perform patriotic character-building activities. Theatre managers worked closely with the merchants who sponsored the clubs. Sponsoring businesses included local bakeries that offered cakes to youngsters on their birthdays, dairies that gave away free ice cream, florists who sent bouquets to sick club mem-

bers, department stores that delivered cheap toys or paper Mickey Mouse masks to encourage the buying of more expensive children's items, and banks that gave out small, metal dime savings banks that had Mickey color lithos on their fronts. In 1932 the club had over a million members in the United States with branches in England as well. The Odeon Theatre chain in Great Britain, which operated 160 theatres, attracted over 100,000 children each Saturday through the Mickey Mouse clubs.

Among Mickey's many fans was England's Queen Mary, who once refused to leave a film performance

Sheet music: "Mickey Mouse's Birthday Party," 1936. © Walt Disney Productions.

1. Detail of glass and chromium cocktail tray painted on reverse in Jazz Moderne pattern, c. 1930. See illustration of complete tray on page 13. Photograph: Helga Photo Studio, New York.

2. "Three Little Pigs" beer-parlor tray celebrating the repeal of Prohibition, color lithograph on metal, 1933.

3. Wood and glass tray with design created from butterflies' wings, Rio de Janeiro, c. 1939.

4. Floor lamp with beaded silk shade that has been lacquered with glistening powdered glass and decorated with a hand-painted cockatoo, c. 1926.

5. Vat-dyed cotton upholstery and drapery fabric with tropical flower-and-leaf motif, c. 1938. Photograph by Helga Photo Studio, courtesy Second Hand Rose, New York.

6. Art Deco clock in green, red, and ivory Catalin, imported from France, c. 1935. Photograph by Helga Photo Studio, courtesy Primavera, New York.

7. Metal windup mantel clock on marble base from France featuring two Casino de Paris showgirl nudes, signed Limousin, 1925.

8. "Mood" lamp in white metal painted Depression green with showgirl nudes gazing into a green glass fixture, marked Frankart, 1927.

9. White-metal figural lamp with green-bronze finish on marble base by Max Le Verrier, imported from France, 1925.

10. *The Dance Magazine of Stage and Screen* with cover design by José Acosta featuring a dancer resembling Art Deco "greenie" statuettes of the period, October 1930.

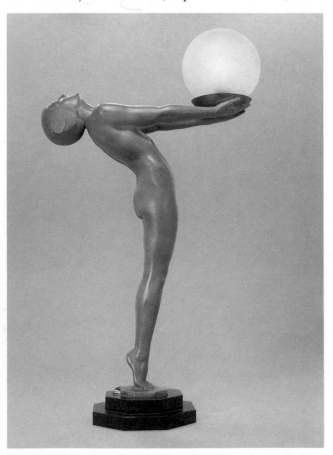

11. Cymbal dancer inspired by Isadora Duncan; imported from France, signed Fayral, 1927.

12. *(above, left)*. Bronze statuette with Moderne features inspired by Gertrude Lawrence, on onyx base, by Lorenzl; imported from France, c. 1931.

13 *(above, right)*. Covered vase in green milk glass, McKee Glass Company, 1934.

14 *(right)*. Vase in skyscraper style with seventeen openings for flowers; marked Germany, c. 1930.

15. Hand-painted dinner plate in the Sunburst pattern; import from J. Maddock & Sons, England, late 1920s.

16. Fiesta ware pottery glazed in South of the Border colors, 1930s–1950s.

17 *(right)*. Fiesta ware advertisement, *Daily News* Sunday magazine supplement, October 1941.

18 *(below, right)*. Block-pattern luncheon set in green Depression glass offered for 59¢ plus $2.00 to join a Larkin Merchandise Club in 1931.

19 *(opposite, above)*. Shirley Temple pitcher and milk mug in blue Depression glass; Honeycomb pattern by Hazel Atlas Glass Company made for distribution as a free premium by Gold Medal Foods, 1935.

20 *(opposite, below)*. Painted kitchen cookie jars: Mickey Mouse, Donald Duck, and José Carioca, made by Leeds China Co., 1947. © Walt Disney Productions.

21 *(above left)*. Glazed ceramic wall plaque from Czechoslovakia, c. 1933.

22 *(above, right)*. Art Deco talcum tins, late 1920s.

23 *(right)*. Combination dry rouge-and-powder metal compact sold at drugstore cosmetic counters and at Woolworth's—painted in sunburst and geometric design, marked Deere, c. 1929.

24 *(above, left)*. Tangee powder box with large Deco flowers, 1930s.

25 *(above, center)*. Princess Pat rouge case in "tango" orange, a fashionable color of that time, c. 1928.

26 *(above, right)*. Tangee powder box with striking curved motifs, late 1930s.

27 *(left)*. Cloth-covered cardboard cosmetic or jewel case from Woolworth's, c. 1925.

28 *(below)*. Painted celluloid pin with paste stones that sold for 15¢ at Woolworth's in 1933.

29. Rudy Vallee and his protégée, singer Alice Faye, 1935.

30. Snow White and the Seven Dwarfs Emerson table radio in pressed Syroco wood; the retail price in 1938 was $14.95. © Walt Disney Productions.

31 (*above*). Catalin "plug-in" portable Fada "Baby" radio in the aerodynamic "teardrop" style, c. 1934.

32 (*left*). Little Orphan Annie Secret Society annual membership booklet for 1940; the radio Society originated in 1934.

33. Little Orphan Annie Ovaltine shake-up mug—a radio send-away premium made of Beetleware, 1930s.

34. Radio's Lone Ranger target game, color lithograph on tin from Louis Marx & Co., dated 1938.

35. Radio's Kate Smith lent her name to many products, including the "America" game that she designed herself; made by Toy Creations, Inc., New York, early 1940s.

36. *Motor* magazine, January 1935.

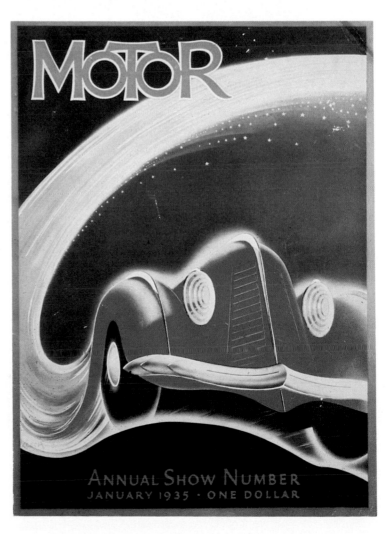

37. Pep Boys "Pure as Gold" motor oil in two-gallon size, color lithograph on tin, c. 1939.

38. Sunday picnic with roadster: English toffee tin from Mackintosh & Sons, Ltd., c. 1926.

39. *The Boy's Story of Lindbergh, The Lone Eagle*, John C. Winston Co., 1928.

40. *Everyday Science and Mechanics*, December 1933, and *Science and Invention*, April 1929.
Two hobby magazines that illustrated new conceptions of speed and travel in futuristic style.

41 *(above, left)*. Mickey Mouse and his pals decorate the cover of *Modern Mechanix*, January 1937. © Walt Disney Productions.

42 *(above, right)*. Mickey Mouse window poster for bread, c. 1934. © Walt Disney Productions.

43 *(below)*. Lionel Train's Mickey Mouse windup handcar that sold for $1.00 in 1934. © Walt Disney Productions.

44. Mickey and Minnie "Helpmate" child's tea set, color lithograph on tin, labeled Ohio Art Co., 1934. © Walt Disney Productions.

45. Depression-green Little Orphan Annie "plug-in" metal stove with electrical coils so that children could heat up their own pot of Ovaltine, 1933.

46. Six examples of Big Little Books featuring Little Orphan Annie, Whitman Publishing Co., Racine, Wisconsin, 1930s.

47. A group of Big Little Books featuring Mickey Mouse and his friends, Whitman Publishing Co., 1930s. © Walt Disney Productions.

48. *Gang Busters*, *Dick Tracy*, *The Green Hornet*, and *Mr. District Attorney* in Big Little Books, Whitman Publishing Co., 1930s.

49. Dick Tracy in action in a pop-up book, Pleasure Books, Inc., Chicago, 1935.

50. "Turkey Deco" terra-cotta panel against a fluted chrome background on a building at Washington and Linden streets, Newark, New Jersey, c. 1931.

51. Art Deco tile decoration on the Austin Manufacturing Co. building, Albany Street and Boulevard, Atlantic City, New Jersey, early 1930s. Photograph: Timothy Bissell.

52 *(above)*. Decorative ceramic tile, 1930s.

53 *(right)*. Decorative ceramic tile, 1930s.

54 *(below)*. Hexagonal neon clock by Attentioneer, manufactured by Neo-lite Corp., Cleveland, Ohio, c. 1938.

55. Official New York World's Fair poster by Staehle, 1939.

56. New York World's Fair painted-glass picture frame with photo of Loretta Young and two sets of Trylon-and-Perisphere salt-and-pepper shakers in Bakelite, 1939.

57 *(left)*. Souvenir matchbook from the New York World's Fair.

58 *(center)*. Billboard poster with sunburst motif advertising Olympic Park in Irvington, New Jersey, 1930s.

59 *(below)*. Painted plaster and chalk amusement-park prizes. Left to right: Charlie McCarthy, Mae West, Betty Grable, Pinocchio, Dopey, and the Lone Ranger, late 1930s and early 1940s.

60. *Movies for the Millions* by Gilbert Seldes, B.T. Batsford, London, 1937.

61. Movie-lobby poster featuring Mickey Rooney and Judy Garland, 1940.

62. Sonja Henie coloring book, Merrill Publishing Co.,
1939.

63. Betty Grable coloring book showing her in *Down
Argentine Way* costume, Whitman Publishing Co., 1941.

64 *(above)*. Large drugstore window-display board for Max Factor cosmetics featuring Ginger Rogers, early 1930s.

65 *(below, left)*. Shirley Temple on the cover of *Photoplay* magazine, January 1935.

66 *(below, right)*. Lupe Velez, the "Mexican Spitfire," on the cover of *Silver Screen*, December 1932.

67. Two magazine covers showing the movies' inimitable platinum blonde, Jean Harlow, illustrated on *Jean Harlow's Life Story*, 1937, and on *True Story*, April 1931.

68. Clara Bow, who once drove down Hollywood Boulevard in a red Packard convertible with twenty chow-chows that matched her flame-colored hair, is seen on this cover of *Motion Picture*, November 1932. William Randolph Hearst's mistress and protégée, the gifted comedienne Marion Davies, is shown on *Movie Classic* for December 1932.

69. Novelized movies from 1920s, 1930s, and 1940s featuring stars Dorothy Lamour, Jean Harlow, and Joan Crawford on the dust jackets.

70. Metal outdoor Coca-Cola sign featuring "Betty," the Coke girl, dated 1941.

71. Lucky Strike cigarette and tobacco tins, cartons, and packages, 1930s.

72. Metal cigarette sign with Philip Morris's famous bellboy, c. 1947.

73. Lux, Rinso, Oxydol, and Gold Dust were some of the most popular soap powders used in the 1920s, 1930s, and 1940s.

74. Large three-dimensional store display sign featuring the famous Gold Dust twins, late 1920s.

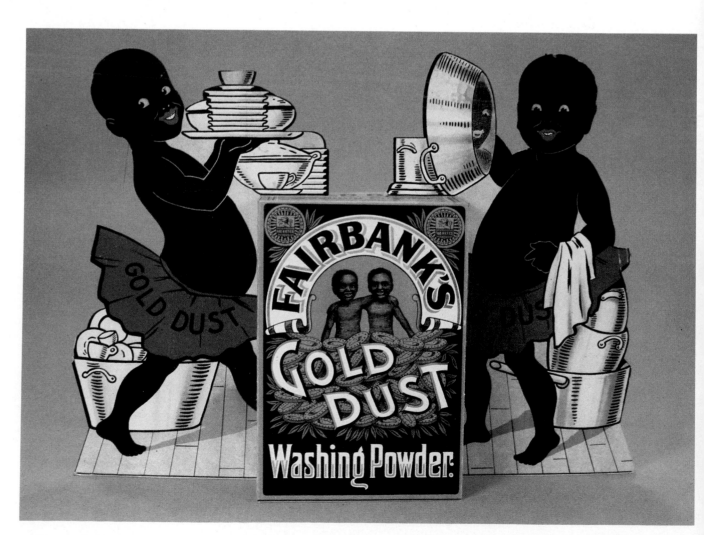

Mickey Mouse Comic Cookies: a cardboard hat sendaway made by Nabisco, Inc., 1933. © Walt Disney Productions.

until she saw the Mickey Mouse cartoon, even though her ladies-in-waiting were imploring her to hurry to a high tea at the palace for which she was already tardy. Franklin and Eleanor Roosevelt were special Mouse fans, always screening a Mickey cartoon in the White House, as was "America's Sweetheart," Mary Pickford, who said in an interview that Mickey was her very favorite star. Charles De Gaulle was also an admirer, and collected Mickey Mouse artifacts during most of his life.

Million-Dollar Mouse

So immensely popular was the image of Mickey Mouse in the early 1930s that scores of manufacturing firms began to inundate Disney with requests to use Mickey as a logo to promote their products. The lively presence of Mickey on an item helped to ring up more sales on the cash register. Somehow, a beaming mouse who seemed oblivious to the Depression opened the doors of fortune and success for those who hired him. A 1935 merchandising flyer from Walt Disney Enterprises called Mickey Mouse the world's greatest salesman and boasted about his ability to sell $35 million worth of merchandise in one year.

The first Mickey merchandising deal occurred in 1928 when Walt Disney was visiting New York. A mysterious man had been shadowing him on the street. Then he suddenly appeared at Disney's hotel room door, and flashed $300 in cash in front of him as payment for the use of Mickey Mouse on a school notebook. Disney, in need of immediate funds gave his permission to go ahead on the spot, without inquiring about future percentages or profits. This incident, however, made Disney aware of Mickey's merchandising potential, and shortly thereafter he and his collaborator, Ub Iwerks, submitted a trial newspaper comic strip based on Mickey's adventures to King Features, which made its formal debut on January 13, 1930. In 1931 Disney offered a free "autographed" picture of Mickey through the strip, and received requests by the thousands for this first Disney mail giveaway.

A legitimate merchandising contract was signed in 1930 with the George Borgfeldt Company, whose first product was a box of Mickey and Minnie Mouse handkerchiefs. A year later Borgfeldt had many Mickey toys on the market, including a drum, a sparkler, wooden squeak-toys, a jointed wood and composition Mickey Mouse, four velvet dolls, a shooting game, two stencil sets, and a Mickey rubber ball. Bisque figurines of Mickey and other Disney characters were mass-produced as colorful bathroom toothbrush holders that reminded youngsters to brush their teeth, and also in various sets featuring Mickey and Minnie playing musical instruments, canoeing, sitting on an overstuffed couch with the dog Pluto, or separate pieces of Snow White and all Seven Dwarfs, Goofy, Horace Horsecollar, Donald Duck, Ferdinand the Bull, and others. Manufactured in Japan for the Borgfeldt Company, these bisques were found in five-and-dimes, department stores, as prizes in amusement park penny arcades, or sitting on top of gumdrop candies wrapped in colored cellophane and ribbon at the local candy stores and ice cream parlors. A 1934 trade advertisement of the Borgfeldt Company read:

The American public has established an amazing demand for these miniature bisque dolls of the Disney characters. Children, of course, can't get enough of them to play with and grown-ups are calling for them to be used as favors, bridge prizes, and sophisticated decorative touches for the living room, sun room, and den. Any store showing this line in several departments will re-order constantly.

Disney soon found it necessary to hire someone to watch over his interests in the area of "mouse merchandising," and in 1932 he employed Herman "Kay" Kamen, a top promotional man, to be Mickey's sole advertising representative. After forming a corporation to handle Disney's comic characters, Kamen began granting licenses to manufacturers for their products, which included Mickey as a figurine made of wood, metal, rubber, celluloid, china, glass, papier-mâché, or cardboard, and his image on textiles, chocolate candy, and a number of other foods. The corporation demanded quality merchandise and refused licenses to makers of inappropriate products like beer, cigarettes, or laxatives. Design approval on Mickey

Painted-bisque Mickey Mouse toothbrush holder with one movable arm and a bisque figurine of Pluto the Pup, both distributed by George Borgfeldt Co., 1935. © Walt Disney Productions.

Mickey Mouse composition book made by Powers Paper Co., Springfield, Massachusetts, 1935. © Walt Disney Productions.

drawings to Disney's specifications was also required to avoid corrupting the look of the famous mouse. Other corporations were formed to supervise rigidly the manufacturing ethics and advertising methods of the licensees. Disney-Kamen offices in New York, London, Paris, and other cities made certain that products were legitimate and of good quality, and that prices were upheld with no sales cuts or markdowns. By 1934 more than eighty companies used Mickey Mouse, the Three Little Pigs, or some other Disney character to sell their wares. Mickey Mouse had become Big Business.

In 1930 dollmaker Charlotte Clark was hired by Disney Enterprises to produce stuffed Mickeys. Because her output was too slow for the increasing demand, Disney released a sewing pattern through *McCall's* magazine. The package cost thirty-five cents by mail and contained twenty-seven pattern pieces. The sewing instructions suggested that Mickey dolls be made from either cotton broadcloth or flannel. These patterns were sold from 1932 to 1939 and included a notice stating that they could not be sold commercially, although many industrious seamstresses in the Depression ignored this warning, making the dolls in quantity and accepting "donations" from the many who wanted one. A contract to produce Mickey, Minnie, Donald Duck, and Big Bad

Wolf dolls was offered to the Knickerbocker Company; and these finely executed pieces were made of cloth and wood. The Seiberling Latex Products Company of Akron, Ohio, produced excellent hard rubber dolls of Mickey, Donald, the Three Little Pigs, and the Big Bad Wolf, which resulted in voluminous sales in five-and-dimes across America.

The most popular use of the mouse image was the famous Mickey Mouse comic-character watch first produced by the Ingersoll-Waterbury Clock Company of Waterbury, Connecticut, in mid-1933. Priced to retail at $1.39, it was originally made from World War I Army-surplus watches. Macy's sold 11,000 of these watches, packaged in handsomely designed orange boxes, the first day of their release. Between June 1933 and June 1935 two and one half million were sold, and by 1939 a mouse on a watch had become so much a part of popular American mythology that one was permanently sealed in a time capsule at the New York World's Fair. In 1957 creator Walt Disney himself was presented with the twenty-fifth million Mickey watch. Ingersoll produced a Three Little Pigs wristwatch in 1934 with a ferocious Big Bad Wolf with animated opening and closing jaws chasing three frightened little pigs around the dial, and a Donald Duck wristwatch in 1936, although neither of these enjoyed the enormous sales of the

Mickey Mouse figure in celluloid with movable arms and legs, c. 1933. © Walt Disney Productions.

Hard-rubber Mickey Mouse with movable head made by Seiberling Latex Co., c. 1935. © Walt Disney Productions.

"Mickey the Cowboy" stuffed doll made by Knickerbocker Toy Co., Inc., 1936. © Walt Disney Productions. Photograph by Helga Photo Studio.

mouse watch. Windup or electrical alarm clocks of many of Disney's characters were marketed, with striking designs such as those originally produced by the Bayard Company in 1936. Following the Mickey Mouse lead in the comic-character watch market were Orphan Annie, Buck Rogers, Popeye, Betty Boop, The Lone Ranger, Dick Tracy, and a bevy of other American cartoon favorites. In the late 1940s and 1950s watches also featured the cowboy folk heroes Hopalong Cassidy, Roy Rogers, Gene Autry, as well as the TV puppet cowboy Howdy Doody; but Mickey will always be remembered as the first and foremost in Watchland.

The Lionel Corporation publicly thanked Mickey Mouse for pulling them out of receivership and saving them from bankruptcy during the Depression. In May 1934 the company began manufacturing action-toy handcars to attract the 1934 Christmas season shoppers. With painted composition figures of Mickey and Minnie that moved up and down while the little handcar glided along the tracks under and around the Christmas tree, these attractive toys were an instantaneous success. Lionel received 350,000 orders for the toy, but was only able to make 235,000 in the first year. Because of the demand for the Mickey Mouse handcar, Lionel also put on the market a Donald Duck and Pluto-in-the-Doghouse handcar, an

Seiberling hard-rubber Donald Duck with movable head, c. 1935. © Walt Disney Productions.

The first Mickey Mouse Ingersoll watch with chrome-plated wristband, shown with the original bright orange, black, and white box, 1933. © Walt Disney Productions. Photograph by Helga Photo Studio.

Easter Bunny handcar, and a Santa handcar that had a small Mickey peering out of Santa's sack. No toy had ever had the enormous success of the Mickey-Minnie handcar, and *Fortune* magazine, in its March 1935 issue, offered special congratulations to Mickey Mouse for saving the Lionel Corporation.

The National Dairy Company hired Mickey to sell its ice cream and cheese products, and an affiliate company called Southern Dairies made Mickey Mouse ice-cream-in-a-cup, which sold an impressive six million cups in its first five weeks of sales. A Mickey Mouse soda pop enjoyed popularity on the West Coast and Donald Duck Bread, Mickey Mouse Bread, Donald Duck Orange Juice, Donald Duck Coffee, Mickey Mouse Chocolate Bars, Mickey Mouse Candy Hearts, jujubes (molded into Disney figures), Mickey Mouse gum, and Mickey Mouse butter creams became new fads. National Biscuit Company produced Mickey Mouse cookies and there were also Mickey Mouse jams or marmalades to serve with them. Also, you could eat in style with sterling silver Mickey

Windup alarm clock with a nodding head made by Bayard in France, 1936. © Walt Disney Productions.

Wrapper from 5¢ Mickey Mouse candy bar made by Wilbur-Suchard Chocolate Company, Philadelphia, 1930. © Walt Disney Productions.

"Snow White and the Seven Dwarfs" glass tumbler given as a premium by National Dairy Products, 1938. © Walt Disney Productions.

Mouse forks, knives, and spoons from William Rogers and Son or International Silver Company, who produced cups and bowls as well. Many pottery and fine porcelain companies made Walt Disney dishes.

Other advertisers such as General Foods' Post Toasties, Parkay Margarine, and Armour Ham soon joined in the rush to employ Disney characters to help generate sales. Pepsodent Toothpaste, Nu-Blue Sunoco Oil, Royal Typewriter, Super Suds, Camay Soap, and RCA Victor Company, all leased a Disney character to market their wares. The top washday soap company, Procter and Gamble, offered Mickey Mouse masks and Snow White drinking glasses along with their products. Indeed, there seemed to be no product that either Mickey or one of his family of friends could not sell. With so much commodity diversification, Kay Kamen was obliged to create annual Walt Disney merchandise catalogues in conjunction with the toy manufacturers, which they then sent to their many store outlets.

On May 28, 1934, five of the most famous babies in the world were born in Callander, Ontario—the Dionne quintuplets. By 1935 it was reported internationally that the favorite toys of the five identical little girls, Yvonne, Annette, Cecille, Emilie, and Marie, were their celluloid Mickey Mouse baby rattles. In the American Mickey Mouse tradition the Canadian quints went on to merchandise everything in the international marketplace from Karo Syrup to margarine and soup.

Kay Kamen introduced and produced the first official *Mickey Mouse Magazine* in 1933. It was distributed through department stores selling Disney merchandise or at movie theatres showing Disney cartoons. Later, it was also released through dairies, finally gaining national syndicated distribution on the newsstands. Featuring stories, cartoons, comics, and crossword puzzles, it also offered full-page ads for Mickey Mouse toothpaste, Mickey Mouse bedroom slippers, or the Mickey Mouse Noma Christmas-tree lights that featured decals of Mickey and his pals in holiday scenes appliquéd on colored Beetleware

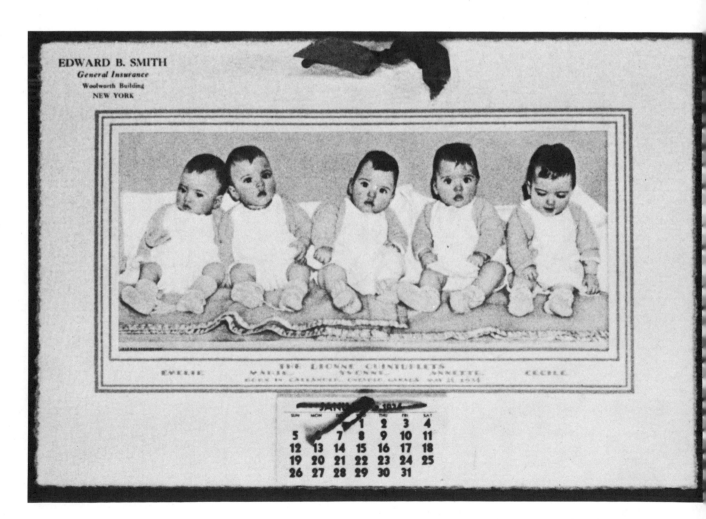

The Dionne Quintuplets calendar, 1936.

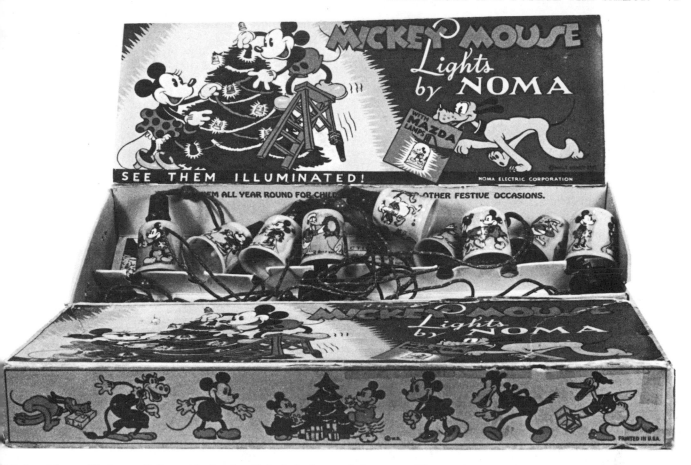

Mickey Mouse Christmas lights with decal celluloid shades made by Noma Electric Corporation, 1936. © Walt Disney Productions.

shades. Anyplace you turned and looked, there was a grinning Mickey Mouse. Even in the more remote lands—Russia, Outer Mongolia, Zambia in Africa, Bulgaria, or Egypt—primitive icons have been found in the image of Mickey Mouse, representing pure Americanism to people that had little or no direct contact with our culture. The phenomenal story of Mickey and Walt, which had its roots in the Great Depression, is a purely American fable that now has become a permanent part of the pop heritage and folklore of the world.

Betty Boop and Popeye the Sailor

Disney's chief competitors in the world of the animated cartoon were Terrytoons, Warner Brothers' Merrie Melodies and Looney Tunes, which presented Bugs Bunny, Elmer Fudd, and Porky Pig, Walter Lantz who reinterpreted Disney's original Oswald the Rabbit, and Max Fleischer who was under contract to Paramount Pictures. Of these, Max Fleischer

The Big Little Book featuring Betty Boop, 1934.

certainly can be said to hold his own alongside Walt Disney so far as imagination, creativity, raw talent, technical skill, and innovation in animation are concerned. Fleischer's *Out-of-the-Inkwell* cartoons, when seen today, have a fresh appeal, awareness, and immediacy that are at once hilarious, sophisticated, and profound.

The main comic character Fleischer created that became a favorite with the public in Depression days was Betty Boop, who was modeled after the famous "Boop-Oop-a-Doop" girl, Helen Kane, a Broadway and recording star and also a contract player at Paramount. A great deal of friction existed between Max and Helen over cartoon-star Betty; and Helen even managed to bring suit against Fleischer claiming she was the only one who should legally be permitted to "boop-oop-a-doop" all day. Max and his cartoon protégée were cleared in the courts, and the job of Betty's baby-doll voice in films and radio went to Mae Questel who could "boop-oop-a-doop" with the same childlike exuberance as Helen.

Betty Boop's first appearance in Fleischer's Talkartoons (1930) was in *Dizzy Dishes*, which had a more canine than human Betty performing as a nightclub entertainer. Her second appearance was in *Barnacle Bill* with Bimbo the Dog, another famous Fleischer character who, along with Koko the Clown, became regular sidekicks for Betty. By 1932 in *Any Rags* Betty's cartoon form had become more fully humanized with her large kewpie head resting, seemingly without the support of a neck, on a petite but shapely frame and her legs were as good as any Zieg-

feld Follies chorine. Betty, the pert, mirthful little flapper, somewhat of a holdout from the 1920s jazz age, soon became the Fleischer trademark for his *Out-of-the-Inkwell* series. *Minnie the Moocher*, which combined an animated Betty with a live-action Cab Calloway and his band, was Betty's first big hit; and other popular black-and-white Fleischer shorts were the "follow the bouncing ball sing-alongs" featuring Ethel Merman and jazzman Louis Armstrong, and the all-animated *Betty Boop for President* (1932), *Snow White* (1933), and *Betty in Blunderland* (1934). Betty Boop's image also moved into the merchandising market and she was prominently featured on soap, handkerchiefs, playing cards, tea sets, toy ukuleles, cigarette cases, compacts, scarves, pins, pajamas, perfume bottles, school notebooks, candy bars, and plaster, celluloid, bisque, and wood-jointed dolls, on The Big Little Books, and there was also a Betty Boop radio.

Popeye the Sailor gained nationwide exposure in the 1930s when he was developed by Fleischer as a character in his animated cartoons. Originally, Popeye came out of Elzie Segar's syndicated comic strip *Thimble Theatre*; but he captivated the world on celluloid in his first appearance in a cartoon called *Popeye the Sailor*, which also featured Betty Boop and Olive Oyl, Popeye's official girl friend, as well as Wimpy, the hamburger eater. Popeye fulfilled the national ideal of tough superstrength masculinity with his corncob pipe and hard-boiled seafarer's slogan "I yam what I yam an' tha's all I yam." This existen

Painted bisque Betty Boop figures shown with her sidekicks Koko the Clown and Bimbo the Dog, Fleischer Studios, 1934.

tial approach to life appealed to Americans who identified with Popeye's ability to take direct, gruff action against his adversaries, after getting his explosive strength from the famous can of spinach. The many Popeye plaster dolls, cutouts, Popeye lamps, and countless other Popeye-endorsed products were inspired by the Fleischer cartoons and earned creator Segar over $2,000 a week at the height of the Depression.

After Disney's phenomenal success with *Snow White*, Paramount prevailed upon Fleischer to produce a feature-length cartoon, and he gave them the colorful *Gulliver's Travels*, which was a success when it opened at Christmastime in 1939. A second color cartoon feature, *Mr. Bug Goes to Town* (1941), was an artistic, although not a commercial, success for Fleischer. It lacked the fluidity and scope Disney was bringing to animation by 1940 with highbrow feature films like *Fantasia*, which combined symphonic music and animation for the first time.

Depression Orphan

Little Orphan Annie was another comic character to emerge as an important symbol for the Depression years. Annie, created by Harold Gray, was renowned as a radio and comic-strip star but never appeared in an animated film though two live-action movies were made—one by RKO in 1932 which starred Mitzi Green, the other from Paramount in 1939 which featured Ann Gillis. The Orphan Annie syndicated newspaper comic strip first appeared in 1924, and its

Popeye the Sailor "Idealite" lamp in painted white metal, marked King Features Syndicate, Inc., 1935.

Box for Little Orphan Annie Game, 1927.

readership reached sixteen million with a continuing wide circulation until just recently. A legacy of the Coolidge era, Annie's chief formula during the 1930s and 1940s was the preservation of a positive spirit and innocence, sustained through perseverance, hard work, and hard-earned dollars, that could help keep America "safe for democracy" during lean times. A store clerk in one of the Annie strips said about her: "What a youngster—just a kid; yet in some ways, she's a thousand years old—having to shift for herself has made her wise beyond her years, yet it hasn't soured or spoiled her—she has the right stuff in her." Her two blank, egg-shaped eyes seemed to offer a vacuity into which readers could project their own meanings, and her frizzy, orange locks were no less famous than Shirley Temple's yellow sausage curls. The image of the little homeless waif, Annie, her nose pressed against a frosted windowpane, gazing longingly at the warm crackling fire inside a happy family's cozy living room as heavy winter snow fell onto her and the big dog Sandy, captured the emotions of innu-

merable Americans, many of whom were abandoned, without shelter, hopeless, and standing in breadlines.

In the first *Little Orphan Annie* Big Little Book (1933) we find Annie in one of her typical situations:

"Leaping lizards," said Orphan Annie, peering into the sugar bowl. "No sugar and no cream. Well, we'll just have to get along without. I guess it won't be the first time, will it, Daddy Warbucks?"

Little Orphan Annie moved busily about the little kitchen—first to the stove, then to the pantry, then to the table. Daddy Warbucks watched her with a wistful smile on his face. He loved the little orphan girl whom he had taken into his home when he was rich. Now that he had lost everything he owned on the stock market, he was finding it hard to take care of her.

"Poor little tyke!" he thought. "She's got some hard days ahead of her before better times. Still, perhaps, I ought not to feel too sorry for the kid. She always manages in some way to get the best out of everything."

Board for Little Orphan Annie Game, made by Milton Bradley Co., 1927.

These "gangbusting" Big Little Books sold for a dime each during the Depression.

Captain Marvel, Mickey Mouse (© Walt Disney Productions), and Superman dime register banks, late 1930s and early 1940s.

"Now, Daddy, supper's almost ready," said Orphan Annie. "You just move your chair to the table while I pour the coffee, an' we'll be all ready for supper in a jiffy."

"It certainly smells good, Annie," said Daddy Warbucks, as she filled his cup.

"And it's going to taste good, too," said Annie. "You know, Daddy, ever'thing tastes better when a body doesn't have too much to eat . . ."

Big Little Books

Few things represent the "feel" of the 1930s more than a Big Little Book. Big Little Books were small, thick, children's books with pictures, which were "novelized" from the comic strips, radio shows, or movies. They usually measured about four and a half inches by four inches and were about one and a half inches thick, often running over 300 pages, and were designed to fit snugly into Junior's jacket pocket, schoolbag, or lunch box. These books were sturdily constructed and depicted on their brightly colored cardboard covers the kids' favorite characters, which might have included Mickey Mouse, Orphan Annie, Dick Tracy, The Lone Ranger, Tom Mix, Judy Garland, Mickey Rooney, Shirley Temple, Jane Withers, and many others. Receiving one under the Christmas tree or on a birthday was always a special treat for youngsters, who couldn't get enough of them. The Whitman Publishing Company issued over 400 titles in the Big Little Book series and also produced coloring books, scrapbooks, and paper-doll cutouts. Competitors in the Big Little Book market in the 1930s were Fast Action Books from Dell Publishing, Dime Action Books from Fawcett Publications, Five Star Library and Little Big Books from Saalfield Publishing Company. In the late 1930s Whitman changed the name from Big Little Books to Better Little Books. Any of these could be bought at Woolworth's during the Depression for a dime; and they were often a child's introduction to the "novel" form. Dick Tracy was the first character to appear on a Big Little Book in 1932. The heyday of the Big Little Books was from 1933 to 1949, although they enjoyed their greatest popularity in the 1930s and are mostly associated with that decade.

The first genuine American comic book was *Funnies on Parade*, which hit the newsstands and candy stores in 1933. David McKay began publishing *King Comics* in 1936; but the ten-cent pulp comic had to wait until the late 1930s and early 1940s to gain a wide circulation. *Action Comics*, Number One, which presented Superman for the first time, appeared in June 1938. In the 1940s two million *Captain Marvel* comic books were printed every two weeks, and new characters were constantly being added to the roster of comic-book heroes in that decade. Wonder Woman, Captain America, Daredevil, Bullet-Man, Green Lantern, the Human Torch, Hawk Man, The Flame, Blue Bolt, and Mary Marvel were just a handful of these phenomenal fantasy beings. The comic book superseded the Big Little Book in popularity by World War II, because not only could they be read faster but also they were cheaper to produce for a mass market.

Other notable children's books were the "pop-up" series first published in 1932 by Blue Ribbon Books, Inc., which brought well-known comic characters into three-dimensional pop-up pictures. Orphan Annie, Dick Tracy, Popeye, Buck Rogers, Tarzan, Flash Gordon, Terry and the Pirates, Mickey Mouse, Minnie Mouse, and a host of Disney Silly Symphony characters all "popped up" in action scenes when the book was opened and vanished when it was closed.

Mary Marvel comic book, Fawcett Publications, 1946.

Captain Marvel whizzing around the Empire State Building on the cover of *Captain Marvel Adventures*, May 1947.

5. FACADES AND ODDITIES

Art Deco Skyline

America's main contribution to the advancement of modern architecture is the skyscraper. When the great monolithic concrete-and-steel structures like the Chrysler Building (1930) and the Empire State Building (1931) first jutted into the skies, the concept of modernity appeared in a startling new reality. New York, which had more skyscrapers than any other city in the world, became the foremost example of the kind of "wonder city" that was depicted in the visionary drawings by Hugh Ferris in his book *The Metropolis of Tomorrow* (1929). The Chanin Building, Rockefeller Center, and the RCA Victor Building, each with its own unique Art Deco facade and interior, helped make New York the world capital of modern architecture.

The first Art Deco skyscraper in New York under construction in 1923, prior to the 1925 Paris Exposition, was the Barklay-Vesey Building. This was designed by McKenzie, Voorhees, and Gmelin as an equipment and administrative center for the New York Telephone Company. The Bell Telephone Company, which was expanding its communications systems with great rapidity in the 1920s and 1930s, was the first to erect many new office buildings in cities across America in a specifically Art Deco style. One classic example is the New Jersey Telephone Company Building in downtown Newark, designed by Voorhees, Gmelin and Walker, which features on its exterior cast-cement floral motifs and stylized human figures "talking" into telephones, while the immense lobby combines decorative terrazzo wall panels, ornate bronze torch lamps, bronze grilles, and gleaming marble walls, creating a total effect reminiscent of the mammoth sets used by Cecil B. De Mille in his early biblical films.

As America struggled through the Depression, this new architecture, which focused on jazzy ornamentation fused into the design of solidly constructed buildings, began to appear in cities and towns across the land. The use of bronze, brass, cast iron, copper, lead, zinc, tin, nickel, steel, aluminum, monel, and

New York City guide magazine, 1936.

78

other metals for decorative purposes was an innovation of this early modern architecture. Mosaics, molded and colored tiles, glazed terra-cotta, travertine, brick, and other similar materials were also employed in decorative bands around buildings or in motifs strategically placed at entrances, on caps of buildings, and in spandrels between windows. Zigzag, triangular and declinate patterns, waves, or the Egyptian ziggurat were used freely on facades, as were exaggerated fruit and floral motifs, vegetable cornucopia, animals, fish, wildfowl, or Moderne style classical godlike figures of Zeus, Mercury, or Diana the Huntress. Special attention to detail in the interior design of a building included everything from mailboxes to elevators to the furnishings: executive desks, chairs, sofas, lamps, and lobby console tables. New "hidden" fluorescent Lumalite systems were incorporated to give rooms indirect lighting from "invisible" sources, and more expansive effects were created by adding large panels of mirrored glass.

Apartments built in the 1930s using Art Deco moldings on their facades gave individuality to what might otherwise have been anonymous structures, while more elaborate apartments such as The Century, The Majestic, or the Eldorado on Manhattan's Central Park West became the new huge living complexes that consolidated Aztec, Mayan, and futuristic design elements directly into the overall construction. The majority of middle-class Americans continued to dwell in older, more traditional houses during the formative years of modernism. The prototype suburban housing being developed by architectural firms was not the new, rounded, solid white, concrete, tile and glass-brick modern dream houses espoused by the Bauhaus school, but the Humpty-Dumpty Gingerbread or Ann Hathaway English-cottage-style homes built of wood, concrete, brick, and slate that had retained favor with homemakers since the 1920s. These bungalows usually had a high slanted roof that peaked over the front door with a tall brick chimney brought directly into

Cast-cement relief sculptures by Edward McCartan on the exterior of the Bell Telephone Company Building, 540 Broad Street, Newark, New Jersey, 1928.

Hersh Towers, 125 Broad Street, Elizabeth, New Jersey.
At left is an Art Deco capital in cast cement, and under
the window at the right the plaque is of molded copper,
1932.

the frontal design. This was the type of solid little "cartoon" brick house that made the Three Little Pigs feel secure from the Big Bad Wolf; and it was the kind of stone, Grimm fairy-tale cottage that most middle-class American families wanted to own. A more exotic architectural fashion for homes was the Spanish Hacienda style, which used ferroconcrete, stucco, and tile, wrought-iron curved gates, and clay-pipe roofing. These were constructed in hot, palm tree, cacti, and orange grove regions like Florida, Southern California, or New Mexico.

Art Deco architecture enjoyed its greatest vogue in the new construction that took place after the New Deal. Civic buildings such as city halls, prisons, high schools, factories, industrial plants, and warehouses used this style and so did bus terminals, railroad depots, and subway stations. Department stores, Woolworth's, and other five-and-dimes in the 1930s began to employ modernistic Mayan fronts to attract their customers. Smaller shops, shoe stores, bakeries, and beauty parlors were redesigned and given new streamlined exteriors by industrial designers like Kem Weber, Paul Frankl, and Russell Wright. Interiors were redone with modish chrome furniture, blue mir-

Interior lobby of the Hersh Towers with Art Deco grill-work, marble, and infinity mirrors, 1932.

Apartment building at 235 East 22nd Street, New York, 1932. The decorative motifs on the facade are made of blue-green and tan terra-cotta.

Terrazzo decorative wall panel from the interior of the Bell Telephone Company Building, Newark, New Jersey, 1928.

Interlocking bronze Art Deco panel from the front door of the Women's House of Detention, Greenwich Village, New York, constructed 1927–1932.

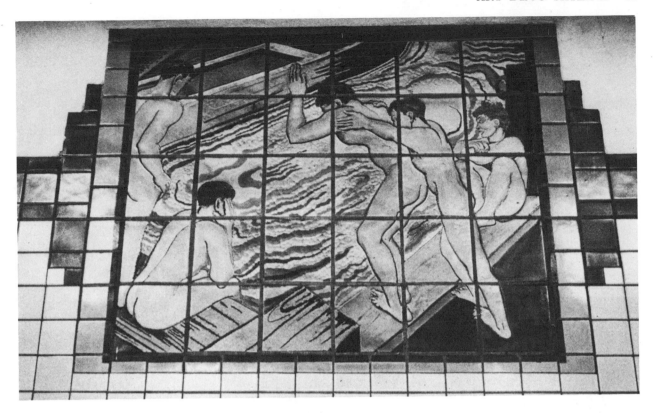

Newark City Subway System. WPA tile mural showing boys swimming, 1935.

Bronze, nickel, and chrome console table, 1930.

Decorative bronze office-lobby grille, c. 1928.

Max's Diner, 731 Harrison Avenue, Harrison, New Jersey, 1925. The exterior is in maroon and cream enamel and wood.

rors, wall-to-wall carpeting, and indirect lighting for a Moderne effect. L. Bamberger's, Newark's largest department store, hired Raymond Loewy, who remodeled the interior, developing new display and showroom techniques to entice the modern-minded shopper.

Pop Architecture

The vernacular of the American pop environment existing in the 1920s and 1930s certainly would include diners, which originally were converted from old railroad cars transported to city sites and became the main eat-in "joints" along the roadside, where you could obtain a cheap meal, a hamburger, a bowl of soup, and a cruller with a cup of coffee. Initially, diners had shiny enamel exteriors with signs spelling out in "Broadway"-type lettering—GUS', FREDDY'S, MILDRED'S, or MAX'S DINER. Usually interiors retained their original railroad-car oak paneling, adding only stainless steel and tile brick for sanitary purposes. Sometimes an overhead whirring ceiling fan, a brightly

colored, lighted coin-operated electronic phonograph machine, and metal Coca-Cola and sandwich advertising signs completed the picture of the American "dream diner." Diners eventually became more elaborate and were prefabricated on factory assembly lines from industrial designs that incorporated chrome, stainless steel, glass brick, along with decorative blue and peach mirrors, achieving what may now be viewed as an ultimate in pop-Moderne architecture. Mammoth neon "Diner" signs and industrial neon octagonal clocks were later added to attract nighttime drivers. Bright-colored neon signs achieved colossal proportions in the 1930s in Times Square with the great sign advertising Wrigley's Chewing Gum, its aquarium fish spouting green and yellow floating bubbles, as well as the huge animated Planter's Mr. Peanut sign; and out on Highway 9 in Newark, New Jersey, the famous red neon Eagle still flaps its wings over the Budweiser brewery.

Most of these extravaganzas were created by neon-sign designer and engineer Jacob Starr, president of Artkraft Strauss Sign Corp., the General Outdoor Advertising Co., or Douglas Leigh, designer of the famous Camels Cigarette sign that depicted a man's head with an animated hand holding a cigarette that moved to and from an open mouth, which "puffed" a continuous stream of giant-sized smoke rings into Times Square to the wonder of the passing crowds.

The White Castle System ("Buy 'em by the sack") opened its hamburger restaurant chain in 1921, spreading infectiously one after the other throughout the country, serving five-cent, tiny, square hamburgers and delicious coffee to millions of Americans. These shining, white-with-black-trim, porcelain enamel and tile eateries were well lit, miniature pop-Gothic castles, and the first of the big-small chains to become popular with the masses. Derivations of the White Castle System turned up in the cities and on the highways, the uniformed waiters serving hamburgers, hot dogs, and coffee; chains like the White Tower, Red Beacon,

Postcard of the Times Square Automat, 1938. All of the Horn & Hardart restaurants were first-rate examples of the Art Deco style.

Bugs Bunny and Porky Pig enjoy hamburgers in a typical American diner, Dell Comics, 1948.

White Castle restaurant in white-and-black porcelain enamel on Westfield Avenue, Elizabeth, New Jersey, constructed in 1930.

Photo from 1920 of Brummer's Ice-Cream Parlor, 731 Grand Street, Jersey City, New Jersey, with Easter chocolates featured in the windows.

The interior of Brummer's as it appears today—amazingly unchanged.

Blue Castle, White Clock System, White Diamonds, the orange-enameled Stewart's Root Beer Stands, and even the early Howard Johnson's with their cottage-style restaurants modernized with neon and glowing tangerine-red tile roofing. Many of these continue to exist today as fascinating architectural oddities.

New York City had its own restaurant chains during the early modern period where you could get satisfying meals at budget prices; Riker's, Bickford's, Rudley's, the Waldorf Cafeterias, and Schrafft's. The Horn and Hardart self-service-Automats, with their coin-operated revolving food servers, gave a new pop sensibility to dining and were an inspiration in modern restaurant technique and design. Adults and children alike were fascinated when, after putting nickels into a slot, the partition containing a sandwich, pie, or other dish of their choice clicked open as if they were participants in a fun-arcade food game in an amusement park. Automats, beautifully designed in the Art Deco manner, were kept spotless and sanitary, offering fresh, inexpensive, home-style foods. Drugstore chains like Walgreen's or Rexall's maintained modernistic lunch counters as did the five-and-dimes, many of them decorated in striking Moderne style emphasizing cleanliness, efficiency, and courtesy.

Bronze fish from wall panel, Hotel Traymore, Atlantic City, New Jersey, 1930.

Handsome sea horse in cast cement that decorates Convention Hall on the boardwalk, Asbury Park, New Jersey, 1928.

A favorite with Americans yesterday and today are the small-town, family-operated ice-cream parlors, which continue to make their own ice cream in addition to homemade chocolate candies. Originally, these parlors were decorated in stained glass, fine carved wood with marble-topped counters; and in the 1930s some of them incorporated the new Moderne fixtures, light sconces, upholstered leatherette booths, and Formica-top chrome tables into their traditional settings, adding the new black glass, neon signs, and modernistic decorative accents to their facades. Some very good examples of these parlors, still intact, can be discovered in small towns and cities, often in an out-of-the-way location, a forgotten or blighted area.

The architecture in old-style seaside resorts such as Atlantic City or Asbury Park, New Jersey, is often quite amazing in its eclectic mix of Art Deco, Art Nouveau, and Moorish modes jumbled into an ostentatious pop style. Convention halls, movie theatres, hotels, and boardwalk taffy and fudge shops all employed exaggerated bloated fish, sleek seahorses, gulls

White Clock System restaurant with coffee-cup tower, Belleville Turnpike, Kearny, New Jersey, 1938.

in flight, reclining mermaids, leaping porpoises, penguins, ships, octopuses, shells, starfish, or the sea-god Neptune as decorative moldings on building facades and cornices.

Architectural pop-Deco oddities left over from the 1920s and 1930s still remain on the landscape of America as unique testimonials to the origins of our commercial image-oriented culture. Building-size coffee cups housing a doughnut-and-coffee shop, a real estate concern in the shape of a battleship, a giant Dixie Cup milkbar, Hollywood's famous Brown Derby nightclub built in the shape of a derby hat, a tavern in Absecon, New Jersey, decorated with a two-story cat in blinking neon, a Gingerbread Castle for children in Hamburg, New Jersey, designed in the 1920s by Joseph Urban, and countless restaurant buildings that resemble big hot dogs or hamburgers—these are only a few of the "fun-house" architectural images that proliferated on the American scene during the prolific era of early modernity.

(We should like to add parenthetically that many architectural "wonders," even those officially designated as "landmarks," disappear, demolished by ball and chain or dynamite just as they are being rediscovered by an interested public. Such was the fate of the Traymore and splendid Marlborough-Blenheim hotels in Atlantic City, which seems to have settled for a gaudy Las Vegas style on its boardwalk.

Indeed, obsessive redecorating and reconstruction of vintage ultra-Moderne stainless-steel diners has done so much damage to the landscape that it might actually be better to remove them entirely. In most instances functionalism and clean sharp line in design give way to a cluttered fieldstone-and-plastic pseudo-Mediterranean hodgepodge, its essential flaws camouflaged by dimly lit imitation Renaissance chandeliers and planters holding dusty synthetic flower arrangements and an overabundance of hanging plants.

Many noteworthy office buildings, apartment houses, movie theatres, beauty parlors, and restaurants originally constructed in the pop-Moderne style, including the "new" White Castle chain, have suffered from cheap plastic renovation, the inevitable excuse being that it is better for business.)

S.S. Flagship furniture store on Highway 22, Union, New Jersey, originally built in the 1930s as a nightclub for the big bands.

6. VISIONS OF UTOPIA

The Great Fairs of the 1930s

Fairs have always existed with the intent of spreading culture, stimulating progress, fostering trade, providing education, and offering entertainment to the many. They have their origins in the ancient marketplace where initially, the impulse to congregate for the purposes of barter and trade began, and also in the religious festivals or feasts where men became cognizant of and examined their position in the universe.

The world's fairs of the 1930s were meant to introduce the achievements of the new technological age, a world made more efficient by machinery. The utopian vision presented by these fairs was dependent on the future good will of men and women whose energies were hopefully directed toward a cleaner, safer, more harmonious, and better world of tomorrow. By and large, the 1930s fairs tended to avoid the social or economic problems confronting the world in that decade; rather they set out to advance the doctrine that machines would free man through labor-saving devices in factories and homes, ultimately offering him the privilege of new leisure, contentment, and creative time.

The first world's fair to introduce this modern theme was the Chicago "Century of Progress" (1933–1934), held on the shores of Lake Michigan to celebrate the city's 100th birthday. Built on 424 acres of land, the public gasped as it viewed the new ultra-modern futuristic architecture that was America's first official introduction to the age of streamlining. Influenced by the Paris Exposition of 1925, which permitted no building that could trace its stylistic origin to classical forms, the Chicago fair had a radical influence on the future of American architecture, the buildings being constructed in a single plane with an eye toward functionalism.

This fair's main proposition was "Advancement Through Technology"; and a large attendance made it a financial success despite the Depression. Income was derived totally from admissions and the rental of exhibition space. Since it was an unsubsidized event, this arrangement became the model for subsequent fairs. The "Century of Progress" featured the world's largest display of electric lighting up until that time. A beam of light from the star Arcturus actuated the switch that turned on the "electrical color," designed by Joseph Urban, flooding the entire fair in an intense "magical spectrum of electricity." A major attraction was the Electrical Building, which focused on man's new fascination with electricity's power and its potential uses. The Travel and Transport Building, the Hall of Science, a reconstructed Mayan Temple, and another edifice that incorporated a section of the Great

Tydol tourist map for the New York World's Fair, 1939.

Sheet music featuring the Trylon and Perisphere of the New York World's Fair, 1939.

Wall of China were the chief monumental structures at the world's fair of 1933. The midway was the center for an amusement section that included Sally Rand in her notorious fan dance as well as extravagant fun rides and toy exhibits.

The California Pacific Exposition (1935), held in San Diego, was a vehicle to stimulate economic recovery in California and the Southwest. It featured Baroque and Spanish Colonial architecture, also employing Mayan and Aztec decorative motifs into the scheme of its overall concept. In 1936 both the Great Lakes Exposition in Cleveland and the Texas Centennial Exposition perpetuated the themes of modernity and progress for a new world. The San Francisco Golden Gate International Exposition opened on February 18, 1939. Called the "World's Fair of the West," it was situated on the specially built 400-acre Treasure Island in the middle of San Francisco Bay. The main theme of this fair was "Culture and Leisure"; and the architecture had a Far Eastern influence, which became a style known as "Pacifica." Held

to celebrate the completion of the Golden Gate and the San Francisco-Oakland Bay bridges, this exposition was one of the most outstanding, colorful, and successful of the period.

The New York World's Fair (1939–1940) was and is still considered to be the most progressive and important fair of the twentieth century. Subtitled "The World's Greatest Showcase," it displayed a television set to the public for the first time; and in the Chrysler Motors Building designed by Raymond Loewy, a Rocketport Exhibit predicted, to the astonishment of the viewers, Sub-Orbital Space Travel as it would occur in the near future. Under its official banner of brilliant orange and blue the New York World's Fair, built on a 1,216-acre site in Flushing Meadow, Queens, opened on April 30, 1939 to celebrate the 150th anniversary of the inauguration of George Washington. All of the major exhibits and buildings housing the products of industry were designed by America's foremost industrial designers, including Donald Desky, Raymond Loewy, Russell Wright, Gilbert Rohde, and Walter Dorwin Teague.

Box of playing cards from "Century of Progress," the Chicago world's fair, 1933–1934.

Guidebook to the Great Lakes Exposition, Cleveland, Ohio, 1936.

New York World's Fair commemorative plate designed by Charles Murphy for Homer Laughlin China Company, 1939.

The theme and main symbol for the fair were the marvelous Trylon and Perisphere, structures designed by Henry Dreyfuss and executed by the architectural firm of Harrison and Fouilhoux. The strongest symbol for an exposition since the Universal Exposition's (1889) Eiffel Tower in Paris, the Trylon was a slender obelisk rising 700 feet, with a connecting Perisphere, a hollow ball 200 feet in diameter that contained Dreyfuss's diorama of a planned community for the future—"Democracity, a World of Tomorrow". The main theme of this fair was "Building the World of Tomorrow," with a focus on the interdependence of man with community and commerce. The fair, divided into seven zones, Amusement and Entertainment, Food, Communications and Business Systems, Community Interests, Production and Distribution,

Transportation, and an International Area, was built at a cost of $155 million and attracted over 60 million visitors.

Among the unique and popular exhibits was General Motors' Futurama, designed by Norman Bel Geddes, in which "Highways and Horizons," a diorama of vast elevated highway complexes traveled by miniature streamlined aerodynamic-styled motor vehicles, gave audiences a presentation of what life might be like in the year 1960, and The House of Jewels, itself a "jewel" of architecture designed by Raymond Loewy, contained a small amphitheatre that displayed a spectacle of rare jewels, millions of dollars worth of diamonds, rubies, emeralds, opals, pearls, and sapphires, that allowed viewers to experience vicariously the thrills of the legendary King Solomon's

Mines. The great symbols of American pop art architecture at the fair were the National Cash Register Building designed by Ely Jacques Kahn, which recorded the fair's daily attendance, and a giant Underwood Master Typewriter, reputedly the largest in the world, weighing 14 tons with each typebar weighing 45 pounds, that typed letters onto stationery measuring 9 by 12 feet with a typewriter ribbon 100 feet long and 5 inches wide. The most prodigious exhibit was the eight-story Railroads on Parade Building, which demonstrated the systems and capabilities of trains, past, present, and future.

Food exhibits were prominent at this fair, called "the most gastronomical"; and among them were Borden's Dairy World, which featured Borden's famous trademark, Elsie the Cow, along with her bullish husband Elmer. The Wonder Bread Bakery Building presented the "wonders" of new baking and packaging methods, while in the Heinz Dome visitors were given a miniature "Heinz" pickle pin as they were lectured to by a mechanized, larger-than-life-

New York World's Fair recipe booklet featuring Elsie, the Borden Cow.

H. J. Heinz Co. synthetic rubber souvenir featuring the "aristocratic" red-tomato man, sold at the Heinz Dome, New York World's Fair, 1939.

size "Aristocratic" Red-Ripe Tomato-Man who also sang jingles about Heinz 57 Varieties of food—home-style soups, oven-baked beans, spaghetti, tomato juice, or pickles—all of which could be sampled by the public. Two huge doughnut restaurants operated by Mayflower, the Doughnut Casino and the Dough-nut Palace, delighted the crowds by offering tasty crullers served with Maxwell House "Good to the Last Drop" Coffee.

The vast amusement complex and entertainment area presented Frank Buck's "Jungleland," a Macy's "Toyland," a streamliner train called the Gimbel's Flyer, Phillips H. Lord's "Crusade-Against-Crime" Gangbusters Building, the Savoy Dance Center featuring a Harlem Jitterbug show, and Life Saver's 250-foot parachute jump, which was later reconstructed at Coney Island. Special aquatic star attractions were Eleanor Holm and Johnny Weissmuller in Billy Rose's Aquacade, a colorful, waterful superspectacle. The World's Fair Amusement Section became the proto-type for Disneyland, Disney World, Great Adventure, and other of today's family-style entertainment meccas.

Two model dream homes were erected according to FHA standards to be vacation homes for more than forty typical American families for a free one-week stay on the fairgrounds. You could tour the exposition in American Express chairs at the cost of $1.00 and eat a hot dog for 10¢, making it in many people's opinions "a rich man's fair." The fair did have five-and-ten-cent restaurants, but the initial 1939 admission cost of 75¢ (reduced to 50¢ in 1940) seemed prohibitive to many, although nothing could keep the crowds away, and then, once inside, most of the exhibits were free.

No other single event produced more souvenir merchandising than the New York World's Fair of 1939–1940. The Fair Corporation licensed 900 manu-facturers on a royalty basis to use the Trylon and Perisphere on 25,000 items of merchandise, including armbands, flags, zipper pulls, pins, hats, compacts, umbrellas, lamps, tables, silverware, clocks, teapots, pepper and saltshakers, commemorative plates, but-tons, playing cards, wall plaques, fancy tapestries, and a World's Fair R.C.A. Victor Syroco-wood radio. Trylons and Perispheres in blue, orange, or white, symbols of a new future, were in profusion in 1939 and 1940, and souvenirs of this fair are still to be found in stores and private collections.

Official 1939 visitor's button, New York World's Fair, 1939.

New York World's Fair playing cards in the official blue and orange colors, 1939.

Aquacade souvenir program, New York World's Fair, 1939.

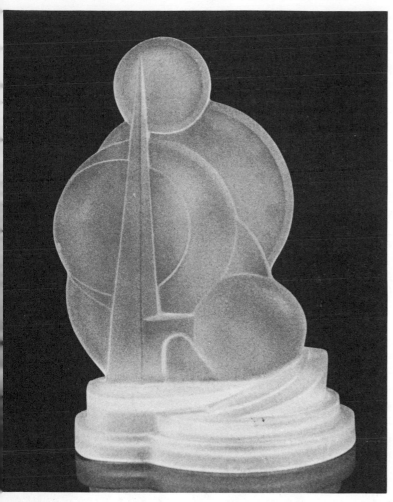

"Mood" table lamp in frosted glass with Trylon and Peris-phere combined with a cloud motif, 1939.

Betty Boop "cocotte"-style, painted-plaster amusement-park doll and pal, c. 1935.

New York World's Fair tea set with blue-on-white decoration, 1940.

One Last Ride on the Merry-Go-Round

Many major cities and smaller towns have nearby amusement parks; but they are fast disappearing. Powerful nostalgia envelops those who remember Coney Island's Steeplechase Park or Dreamland, Palisades Amusement Park, or Olympic Park in Irvington, New Jersey—places that possessed a sense of innocence together with an aura of mystery.

The route to Olympic Park in New Jersey began at the trolley terminal in downtown Newark, which followed the tracks along cobblestoned Springfield Avenue to the end of the line in Irvington, depositing you right at the magical entrance to the old amusement park, a huge white stucco archway bathed in light. The entrance fee was 10¢; and immediately inside was a geyserlike fountain with a revolving rainbow of colored light. To one side of this fountain was an enclosed roller-rink, from which could be heard the faint sound of organ music, and on the other side, a tree-shaded German beer garden with its own brass band featuring Bubbles Ricardo, an ex-trapeze artist turned coloratura soprano. Games of chance or skill surrounded this area, and you might take home as a prize a plaster Popeye, Lone Ranger, Charlie Mc-Carthy, Mae West, Betty Boop or fat Kewpie, brightly painted and pasted with silver glitter. Many middle-class homes of the times displayed one of these prizes on the fireplace mantel or on a bedroom vanity. Nothing evokes the memory of a moldering old amusement park like these simple plaster or chalk statuettes, which were produced in the hundreds of thousands and sold by carnival supply houses to fairs, rodeos, and souvenir stands across the land.

Roaming around Olympic Park, you would pass by a rickety wooden roller coaster and hear screams of terror and delight; a chain-belt conveyor ride called "The Whip"; electric Dodgem cars colliding noisily; astonishing fun houses; giant Ferris wheels; miniature train rides; and the world's largest, most beautifully carved merry-go-round, turning and spinning to a melodious, ancient calliope. For those who enjoyed dark caverns, there was a boat ride through the Tunnel of Love or a venture into the spidery world of a Haunted Castle. Hours could be spent inside a glimmering penny arcade where for 1¢, special coin-operated machines with miniature derricks would pick up and drop candies or a tiny bisque Mickey Mouse into catch trays. At the small open-air circus you would sit on shaky bleachers, gobbling buttered popcorn, 5¢ hot dogs or pink cotton candy, enjoying clown and bicycle acts, dog performers, Hildy's Famous Midget Troupe, trapeze acts, monkeys, wild animals, apes, freaks, stuntmen, jugglers, and many other traveling "carny" acts put up in tents and trailer

homes. Olympic Park, like so many others, also offered "the world's largest outdoor swimming pool." True or not, it was big and refreshing on a hot summer's day.

Many bayside, lakefront, or ocean resorts with boardwalks, piers, pavilions, and enclosed convention halls, fun houses, rides, and theatres like those found on the old Jersey shore at Keansburg, Asbury Park, Seaside Heights, Atlantic City, or Wildwood, and at Rye Beach or Coney Island in New York, still exist and make it possible to enjoy the flavor, color, and atmosphere of the old parks that are so vital a part of the American popular-folk cultural landscape.

Amusement-park ferris wheel windup toy in metal made by J. Chien & Co., Newark, New Jersey, 1947.

Miss America Beauty Pageant program, Atlantic City, New Jersey, 1933.

Saltwater taffy boxes from Atlantic City (1928), New York World's Fair (1939), and Asbury Park (1933).

7. HOLLYWOOD, BROADWAY, AND GOTHAM NIGHT LIFE

Hooray for Hollywood

Silent films had captivated audiences since the early 1900s, and, by the 1910s and the 1920s there was an almost religious fervor in America centered on the epicenter of make-believe—Hollywood. Worshiped by the masses, movie stars were developed and groomed by the studios into grandiose personality images that their fans tried to emulate.

In 1926 the biggest box-office draw was a German shepherd named Rin Tin Tin; and in that same year Rudolph "The Sheik" Valentino died at the peak of his career causing near hysteria in millions of women. Many all-time greats—Charles Chaplin, Mary Pickford, Fatty Arbuckle, Harold Lloyd, Buster Keaton, Lillian and Dorothy Gish, Gloria Swanson, Greta Garbo, Pola Negri, Joan Crawford, Marion Davies, Douglas Fairbanks, John Gilbert, and Ramon Novarro—began as "silents." Directors D. W. Griffith and Cecil B. De Mille attracted millions into movie theatres around the world with stupendous silent spectacles like *The Birth of a Nation* (1915) and *The Ten Commandments* (1923).

Movie critic and film historian Campbell MacCulloch in an article in *Theatre Magazine* (October 1927) reflected on the impact of the early cinema: "No more powerful agency for the transmission of thought and custom has ever existed upon the globe than the motion picture; no greater influence toward uniting mankind has ever been developed." Certainly movies had come a long way from the nickelodeon by that time; but in the same month and year that this article was published, a new phenomenon occurred that was to eclipse the silent film forever: *The Jazz Singer* starring Al Jolson opened on October 6, 1927, in New York at the Warner's Theatre; and Hollywood—and the world—were powerfully thrust into the era of "talking" film with the dynamic Jolson crooning tearfully to his beloved Mammy.

Thomas Edison had synchronized sound with film as early as 1894 with his Kinetophon System—using discs with film—but it was the immense popularity of radio in the 1920s that made the addition of

Accordion-style postcard views of Hollywood, California c. 1935.

Alice Faye with movie camera on 20th Century-Fox lot, 1935. Publicity still.

sound to film a commercial necessity. People were staying at home to listen to radio, and this seriously affected movie box offices; consequently, the entire industry was forced into a new competitive strategy—*sound*. The changeover was swift; and many silent-film stars were unable to make the necessary transition because of poor vocal quality.

The sudden collapse of the stock market cut movie attendance in half just as audiences were being reclaimed with technical advancements in sound film, but the concept of showing a double feature, introduced to theatres in 1931, brought the crowds back into the movie houses. For 25¢ and sometimes less, you could enter your hometown movie theatre, the Ritz, Rialto, Castle, Tivoli, Alhambra, Stanley, or the Rex and see two shows for the price of one. Many of

the theatres were elaborate palaces, sometimes with dark blue "skies" overhead, lit by hundreds of tiny "stars," including "real" moving clouds; some were awash with motifs taken from Chinese pagodas, Persian courts, Egyptian temples, or in the Art Deco style of New York's Radio City Music Hall. The larger theatres featured a Wurlitzer organ that would accompany movie patrons entering and exiting between films.

The first big "All-Talking All-Singing-Dancing" movie that won a "best film" Oscar was *The Broadway Melody* (1929, M-G-M's first sound film), starring Charles King and Bessie Love. Charles Farrell and Janet Gaynor enchanted audiences in the same year introducing the hit tune "If I Had a Talking Picture of You" in the film *Sunny Side Up*. Lavish musicals such as *Hollywood Revue of 1929* with Joan Crawford and Marion Davies, *Paramount on Parade*, or *King of Jazz*, which featured Paul Whiteman and his orchestra, proliferated in the late 1920s and early 1930s attracting record crowds. *Forty-second Street* (1933), *Gold Diggers of 1933, Footlight Parade* (1933), *Dames* (1934), *Flirtation Walk* (1934), or *Shipmates Forever* (1935), all from Warner Brothers and all starring Ruby Keeler and Dick Powell swept away Depression blues as did Eleanor Powell who tap-danced people's cares away while singing melodies like "You Are My Lucky Star" in a series of M-G-M musical extravaganzas including *Broadway Melody of 1936, Broadway Melody of 1938*, and *Broadway Melody of 1940*.

M-G-M offered its huge cinematic musical tribute to Florenz Ziegfeld in *The Great Ziegfeld* (1936), starring William Powell, Myrna Loy, and Luise Rainer; *Ziegfeld Girl* (1941), featuring Lana Turner, Judy Garland, and Hedy Lamarr as Ziegfeld beauties; and *Ziegfeld Follies* (1946) with Fanny Brice, Lucille Ball, and an all-star cast. Showman Ziegfeld himself tried a hand at directing his own lavish movie musical for Paramount, *Glorifying the American Girl* (1929) with Mary Eaton, who closely resembled his stage star Marilyn Miller. Fred Astaire first hit the Hollywood dance floors with Joan Crawford in the elab-

Radio City Music Hall program, 1938.

Gold Diggers of 1933 sheet music with a platinum-blonde Ginger Rogers gracing the cover.

Sheet music from R.K.O. movie *Radio City Revels*, 1937.

Greta Garbo as a comic valentine, c. 1934.

orately produced *Dancing Lady* (1933); and in the same year was joined by a golden-haired Ginger Rogers in *Flying Down to Rio,* which utilized the breathtaking stunt of chorus girls cavorting on the wings of airplanes in flight. The eloquent Fred and a smooth, graceful Ginger became Hollywood's most successful dancing duo and were teamed together in *The Gay Divorcee* (1934), *Follow the Fleet* (1935), *Roberta* (1935), *Top Hat* (1935), *Swing Time* (1936), *Shall We Dance* (1937), and other RKO musical vehicles. Operettas such as *Naughty Marietta* (1935), *Rose Marie* (1936), and *Maytime* (1938) presented the fine singing of Jeanette MacDonald and Nelson Eddy, who were held in special adoration by 1930s American moviegoers.

Usually the 1930s black-and-white movie musicals used fantastic pop-deco sets that had Alice Faye (*Music Is Magic,* 1935) jumping onto the dance floor from inside the dial of a huge radio set, or Ruby Keeler (*Ready, Willing and Able,* 1937) tap-dancing on the keys of a giant-sized typewriter, satisfying audience demand for stupendous, exaggerated, sophisticated, zany, modern musical fantasies. Sets and rooms in 1930s films were decorated in ultra-Hollywood Moderne and gave audiences an intimation of futuristic modern styles as conceived by top designers. Stark, gleaming white walls, lighted curved glass-brick recesses, chromium furniture and ornamentation, as well as reflective glassy black floors for dancing epitomized Hollywood chic and glamour.

The exquisitely beautiful Greta Garbo first "talked" in *Anna Christie* (1930) and became one of the most revered dramatic stars of the 1930s in films like *Mata Hari* (1932), *Anna Karenina* (1935), *Camille* (1937), and *Ninotchka* (1939), adding to her already great silent "mystique" and reputation as an aloof, mysterious embodiment of screen-art perfection. Critics endlessly praised the great Swede whose imperious, remote posture bespoke glamour; and the "Garbo look" changed the fashion standard for American women from a fullsome rounder form to a thin and gaunt frame that also called for pronounced cheekbones, a fuller, painted mouth, pencil-thin highly arched brows, and long, feathery eyelashes. Katharine Hepburn, Marlene Dietrich, and Claudette Colbert each created her own special persona based on the Garbo standard.

By the mid-1930s the use of color in film had been mastered and the first full-length feature to use the Technicolor process was *Becky Sharp* (1935), fol-

Original movie-lobby display in Hollywood Moderne style for the Warner Bros. film *Fashions of 1934,* directed by Busby Berkeley.

Lobby poster for the Hughes-Harlow epic *Hell's Angels,* 1930.

lowed by *A Star Is Born* (1937) with Janet Gaynor and Fredric March, Disney's *Snow White and the Seven Dwarfs* (1938), M-G-M's *The Wizard of Oz* (1939), and the David O. Selznick Civil War epic *Gone with the Wind* (1939). Since color features were expensive to produce, Technicolor was limited during the World War II years chiefly to movie musicals and exotic jungle epics. Betty Grable with her cotton-white hair, American-blue eyes, dark cranberry-red lips, and "million dollar legs" became the servicemen's favorite movie pinup girl in color musicals like *Down Argentine Way* (1940), *Coney Island* (1943), *The Dolly Sisters* (1945), and *Diamond Horseshoe* (1945). Grable became the symbol of the 1940s just as Garbo had represented the 1930s. Her vitality, full whole-some face, girl-next-door image, coupled with the door-slamming cheapness of a hardened chorine made her a pal and a dame the public could love. Never re-mote, basically honest, Betty was the girl who waited at home for the boys to return from the front. Carmen Miranda, the South American Bombshell, with her towering fruit-laden hats, long, painted nails, and high-platform golden wedgies, and a redhead named Maria Montez, America's first Puerto Rican star, who ordered her subjects to leap into a flaming volcano in *Cobra Woman* (1945), became, along with Grable, the reigning "Queens of Technicolor" in the 1940s.

The studio system dominated Hollywood during these years. The big five were Metro-Goldwyn-Mayer, Paramount, 20th Century-Fox, RKO Radio, and Warner Brothers; others included Columbia, Universal, United Artists, Republic, and Monogram, the last two specializing in B movies—crime, horror, and Western—as well as weekly adventure serials, comedies, and band shorts. Usually studios like Warner's, Paramount, and Loew's, Inc. (M-G-M) owned theatre chains, handled distribution, and kept stars under tight, exclusive contracts. The 1930s were the high point for the studio system, and the intense focus on the star personality can never again be as it once was in this decade under the aegis of such movie giants as Louis B. Mayer, Irving Thalberg, Adolph Zucker, Darryl F. Zanuck, Jack Warner, Harry Cohn, Herbert J. Yates, and others. The screwball comedies *It Happened One Night,* starring Claudette Colbert and Clark Gable, and *Twentieth Century* (both 1934), with a screaming Carole Lombard and a volatile John Barrymore, were as much a part of the 1930s mystique as were the dramatic spectacles like the original *King Kong* (1933) with Fay Wray, or Howard Hughes's *Hell's Angels* (1930) which thrust Jean Harlow into stardom. The number of films churned out by the Hollywood machine, inciting the public to spend billions at the box office, is endless—the supernatural horror movies, including *Dracula* (1931) with Bela Lugosi, *Frankenstein* (1931) with Boris Karloff, and *The Cat People* (1942) with Simon Simone, are classics of their genre and instigated a series of first-rate chillers, one following the other in nightmare succession. The Happy Kid Musicals, those that starred Mickey Rooney and Judy Garland, *Babes in Arms* (1939), *Strike up the Band* (1940), *Girl Crazy* (1943), or the Andy Hardy series, have become as much a part of the American culture as apple pie, baseball, and Fourth of July fireworks. Whether it's Myrna Loy and William Powell in *The Thin Man* (1934), or Alice Faye, Tyrone Power, and Ethel Merman in the number-one musical of the 1930s, 20th Century-Fox's Irving Berlin extravaganza *Alexander's Ragtime Band* (1938), this prolific era in film is a relevant place to pinpoint and understand the sociological roots of our early modern popular culture.

Life Inside a Goldfish Bowl

All important to the Hollywood of the 1920s, 1930s, 1940s, and 1950s were the 5, 10, and 25¢ movie fan magazines. The public devoured these gossipy pulp monthlies with a voraciousness that almost rivaled the moving picture itself in their affections. Information about stars and the film world often superseded film criticism; and fans identified personally with the ups and downs of their special favorites. The star system was originally created out of a need on the part of society to worship symbolically perfect human beings; but this situation, more often than not, created a schism between a star's celluloid image and the "human frailties" that persisted just underneath the overt personality that was superimposed by the studios. Movie stars often experienced difficulty in personal relationships due to what columnists insisted was too much acclaim and adoration coming from the public. But this was the price tag of a Hollywood career; and this personal, subjective, vulnerable area is what the fan magazines like *Silver Screen*, *Photoplay*, *Motion Picture*, *Screen Romances*, and *Modern Screen*, or, in particular, Hedda Hopper and Louella Parsons, Hollywood's chief gossipmongers, chose to survey.

A 1933 lyric from a Hollywood song published in *Photoplay* expressed stardom's lament:

Sheet music featuring America's favorites in the late 1930s and early 1940s—Judy Garland and Mickey Rooney.

"The South American Bombshell," Carmen Miranda on *Click*, November 1939.

Screen Romances with Charles Boyer and Greta Garbo, October 1937.

Silver Screen with Ruby Keeler, May 1936.

"LET'S GATHER ROUND THE GOLDFISH BOWL!"

What I eat for lunch, for breakfast;
What I read and what I wear;
How I look when taking sunbaths;
How I get my titian hair—
Why, it's all wide-open knowledge
To the public as a whole,
'Cause there aren't any secrets
In this Hollywood Goldfish Bowl! . . .

Sheet music from film musicals and theme songs from dramatic pictures were a big sideline for the movie industry, but it was the fan magazines that kept the populace in more or less direct contact with the stars. Fan magazines also functioned as "self-improvement" periodicals geared to informing women readers how to emulate their favorite stars. Advertisements in movie magazines reflected this fixation; and they included ads for bust developers, acne cures, underarm deodorants, as well as "Hollywood cosmetics" like blood-red Jungle Savage Lipstick, Marchand's Golden Hair Wash, or Blondex Shampoo,

Maybelline Mascara and lash curlers, all recommended by "The Filmland Experts." Astrology was a favorite of the movie crowd; and frequent references to the forces beyond, often backed up by a gossip columnist's chatty predictions, helped generate the sale of mail-order movie "astro-charts." Other ads usually read something like:

"*I'm awfully fussy about the way my stockings fit,*" *says fascinating Jean Harlow, "*that's why my maid has explicit instructions to wash them—and my underthings too, with LUX.*"*

Or:

"*Life is colorful,*" *says Joan Crawford, "*but even a colorful personality can stand added charm . . . that is where Make-up comes in.*"*

Hollywood stars not only acted in films but were obliged to open supermarkets, pose for endless publicity stills, and appear at the perennial rounds of

These jazzy gossips are part of a bridge-score set, 1932. Photograph by Helga Photo Studio.

Joan Crawford tells it all in *Look* magazine, September 1939.

movie premieres, luncheons, parties, and popular night spots, usually finding rest from this schedule only by manifesting a nervous breakdown. In the April 1936 issue of *Modern Screen* an article by Gladys Hall was headlined: "Jean Harlow Is Jealous of *You*—The World Should Be Her Oyster, But She Thinks You Are the People Who Have All the Luck!" The text read:

> *Jean Harlow is jealous of all you girls, city bred or small town, who lead perfectly normal, natural lives— who do your jobs, close your desk when the work is done, relax, have a good time and are able to forget how your face looks. She is a simple person. And her envy of you other girls is predicated upon one thing— that she is completely natural, and to be forced, however great the rewards, to lead a completely unnatural life just plain gets on the Harlow nerves.*

The December 1932 *Silver Screen* had a feature by Elisabeth Wilson entitled "The Suicide of Her Husband Came Just as the Cup of Happiness Was at

Jean Harlow's Lips." On June 7, 1937, the exuberant Harlow herself succumbed to an untimely death; and innumerable postmortem articles were written in screen magazines blaming it on everything from conjugal problems to Miss Harlow's "peroxided-ammoniated-white-henna-hair." An article in *Photoplay* warned its readers: "Don't Go Platinum Yet—Read Before You Dye." Although Jean Harlow actually succumbed to uremic poisoning, Hollywood created a myth around her death similar to that of Valentino's. Harlow was the prototype of the "Unlucky Blonde Goddess," an image that plagued the lives of other legendary "foredoomed" Hollywood blondes—Carole Lombard, Carole Landis, and Marilyn Monroe—all of whom died in "mysterious" circumstances according to movie-magazine mythology.

Another fan magazine article enticed young readers with: "The Struggle of Joan Crawford to Make Her Way Against Seemingly Insurmountable Obstacles Is the Mirror Reflection of Modern Youth." Joan, whose real name was Lucille LeSeur, was also once known as "Billie" Cassin and was tagged "Joan Crawford" by Mrs. Louis Antisdale of Dallas, Texas, in a 1925 *Movie Weekly* Name-the-Star-Contest, which presented the lucky winner with $1,000. The article develops Joan's atypical struggle up the path to stardom from a five-and-dime countergirl who never really knew her father to chorus girl and flapper, finally arriving in sunny Hollywood, U.S.A., where she became a legendary star, later going on to marry rich Hollywood bachelor actors Douglas Fairbanks, Jr., and Franchot Tone. Joan Crawford became the archetype for "the self-made lady," who had an unhappy and sometimes questionable background. This fascinated her fans who felt that they too might have a chance to "walk her path" if they so chose.

Other movie magazine titles read: "I Want to Fall in Love Again with a Man Like Gary Cooper, Says Lupe Velez," by Gladys Hall (*Motion Picture*, 1932) and "Stars Have to Live Somewhere and Sometimes Their Neighbors Think the Association a Doubtful Honor" by Helen Fay Ludcam (*Silver Screen*, 1935). A lecture on grooming by Sylvia in *Photoplay* (November 1934) advised a rebellious Bette Davis: "An Open Letter to Bette—Beauty and Personality Are Inseparable." The August 1931 issue of *Hollywood Magazine* featured an article entitled "Dolores Del Rio Goes Moderne" by Harry D. Wilson, which described Dolores's changeover from the El Rancho Mexicana Look to an Ultra-Art Moderne Vamp after she married art director Cedric Gibbon. In the story, accompanied with pictures of Dolores in her new Hollywood Bauhaus abode, Senorita Del Rio stated: "I am aching to play the sophisticated roles of modern drama after having been French, Russian,

Indian, Gypsy, Spanish—everything but a Modern." Some articles seem to have been written many times over, changing only the names to suit the occasion: "Will 'Lana,' 'Judy,' 'Hedy,' 'Rita,' 'Marilyn,' 'Greta,' 'Ruby,' or 'Joan' find *real love* this time around?" This was called "life" inside the Hollywood goldfish bowl.

America's Littlest Sweetheart

A pert bundle of corkscrew curls, a mixture of sugar-honey and dynamite named Shirley Temple was by far the most popular star of the 1930s, claiming the title of Hollywood's number-one box-office draw from 1935 to 1938. The appearance of this diminutive ray of sunshine seemed to coincide with the "birth of a new America" in 1934; and the Depression decade that began with a pack of hard-boiled, wisecracking "Gold-Digging Busby Berkeley Dames" ended with a sense of hope and optimism, good humor and innocent charm, which Shirley epitomized for the public. Speaking about Shirley Temple in 1935, Franklin D. Roosevelt said, "During this Depression, when the spirit of the people is lower than at any other time, it is a splendid thing that for just 15¢ an American can go to a movie and look at the smiling face of a baby and forget his troubles." Overnight, she incited mothers to enroll their little girls in tap-dancing schools and to deliver them to beauty parlors where they received a Shirley Temple permanent; and cherubic, dimpled Shirley Temple Dolls, "Shirley"

Shirley Temple Through the Day, The Saalfield Pub. Co., 1936.

cutouts, biographical books, and doll clothing began to be sold in stores across the land. Shirley Temple pictures, which included *Little Miss Marker* (1934; her first big feature, based on a Damon Runyon story), *Baby, Take a Bow* (1934), *Now and Forever* (1934), *The Littlest Rebel* (1935), in which she tap-danced with Bill "Bojangles" Robinson, *Poor Little Rich Girl* (1936) with Alice Faye, and *Heidi* (1937) were made on the average of four a year, grossing $5 million annually, keeping her studio, 20th Century-Fox, solvent during the Depression. Shirley received a miniature Oscar for "bringing more happiness to millions of grown-ups than any child of her years in the history of the world," and she is remembered as "America's Little Sweetheart" singing happy songs like "On the Good Ship Lollipop," "Animal Crackers in My Soup," "That's What I Want for Christmas," and "You Gotta Eat Your Spinach, Baby."

Child stars Deanna Durbin, Jane Withers, Baby Sandy, Judy Garland, and Gloria Jean were also popular favorites in the 1930s, but Shirley was on the cover of more magazines than any other star, child or adult, of the time. In the December 1935 *Silver Screen*, Elisabeth Wilson, in an article entitled, "Give Your Child a Shirley Temple Xmas Party," reported to America the details of a party Shirley's

mother was planning. The varied menu included such children's delights as peanut butter and jelly sandwiches on white Wonder Bread, candied apples, scrambled eggs, hot cocoa, and a marshmallow curly-top cake. Certainly a great number of American children, whose parents could afford it, had a special Shirley Temple Christmas party of their very own that year.

Depression Hits on Broadway

The legitimate Broadway theatre flourished in the late 1920s and the biggest hit was a realistic drama about Prohibition called *Broadway* by George Abbott and Philip Dunning, which opened on September 16, 1926. This play originated the hard-hitting fast-paced journalistic realist school of drama that had an impact on dramaturgical styles in that and succeeding decades.

If you were a New York theatregoer in the 1920s you could attend Eugene O'Neill's *The Emperor Jones* (1920), *The Great God Brown* (1926), or *Strange Interlude* (1928). The musical-comedy entertainments Broadway is most noted for included *Sally* (1920) with an effervescent, golden blonde Marilyn

Sheet music from the Broadway revue *Earl Carroll Vanities, 7th Edition,* directed by Busby Berkeley, 1928.

Shirley Temple in *Wee Willie Winkie,* authorized movie edition, 1937.

The Playgoer, Chicago, 1930.

Katharine Cornell as seen in *The Green Hat* on the cover of *Theatre Magazine,* January 1926.

Shubert Theatre program, New York, 1929.

Miller, *Showboat* (1927), and *The Ziegfeld Follies* of 1927 starring Eddie Cantor and "introducing Ruth Etting" who sang Irving Berlin's "Shaking the Blues Away." *Whoopee* opened in 1928, teaming Cantor again with Miss Etting; and the last *Follies* to hit the boards was in 1931, featuring Harry Richman, Helen Morgan, Gladys Glad, and Ruth Etting all by herself delicately singing "Shine on Harvest Moon," a song originally introduced by Nora Bayes and Jack Norworth in Ziegfeld's 1908 edition of the *Follies.* Miss Etting (see back cover) had achieved her greatest success one year earlier in *Simple Simon* (1930) as the forlorn dance-hall hostess singing the Rodgers and Hart tune "Ten Cents a Dance."

In 1932 a small off-Broadway revue entitled *Americana* introduced the famous Depression song, "Brother, Can You Spare a Dime?" The plea of its refrain, "Why should I be standing in line just waiting for bread?" expressed the collective despair of the millions who were on relief. This song was recorded by everyone, including Al Jolson, Bing Crosby, Russ Columbo, and Rudy Vallee. The economy darkened about half of the theatres after 1929; but some of the outstanding plays seen after the crash were *The Bar-*

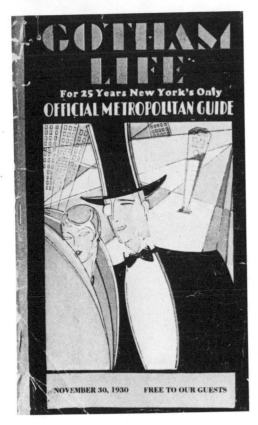

Gotham Life, weekly guide to New York shows, nightclubs, and films, November 30, 1930.

Sheet music for *Wonder Bar,* Andre Charlot's British stage production, 1930.

retts of Wimpole Street (1930) by Rudolf Besier, with Katharine Cornell, *Private Lives* (1930) with author Noel Coward and Gertrude Lawrence, *Tobacco Road* (1933) by Jack Kirkland, *You Can't Take It with You* (1936) by Moss Hart and George S. Kaufman, *Of Mice and Men* (1937) by John Steinbeck, Thornton Wilder's *Our Town* (1938), *The Little Foxes* (1939) by Lillian Hellman, which starred the tempestuous Tallulah Bankhead, *The Time of Your Life* (1939) by William Saroyan. Ethel Barrymore was the first lady of the American theatre, and Noel Coward was then the favorite English import. The Group Theatre created an intellectual stir in New York in the 1930s with a thirty-one-member repertory company that included Lee Strasberg, Harold Clurman, Elia Kazan, Franchot Tone, Frances Farmer, Stella and Luther Adler, and John Garfield. The social protest plays *Waiting for Lefty* (1935), *Awake and Sing* (1935), and *Golden Boy* (1937) by Clifford Odets shook up the complacency of the commercial theatre and called for political and economic changes in the American scheme. The Federal Theatre had the young genius Orson Welles appearing as *Macbeth* with an all-black cast. On the lighter side there was *Face the Music* (1931-1932), a musical that introduced the song "Let's Have Another Cup of Coffee, Let's Have Another Piece of Pie" as its antidote to Depression fears or Olsen and Johnson at the Winter Garden Theatre in *Hellzapoppin* (1938). George Gershwin's *Of Thee I Sing* (1931), Cole Porter's *Gay Divorcee* (1932), and Jerome Kern's *Roberta* (1933) livened up the musical theatre scene; and fanciful operettas such as *The Chocolate Soldier, Blossom Time,* and *The Student Prince* all had successful revivals on Broadway.

Painting the Town Red

If you enjoyed night life and could afford a "hi-hat after-theatre whirl around Gotham" you might "punish the parquet" at the Central Park Casino to the rhythm of Leo Reisman's Orchestra, which offered a jubilant Ethel Merman vocalizing between theatre engagements. Other famous New York hot spots you could hit were the plush, zebra-skin-decorated El Morocco, Sherman Billingsley's Stork Club, Billy Rose's Diamond Horseshoe, and the Kit Kat Club on East Fifty-fifth Street; or you might indulge in a "cheek-to-cheek"

"Cotton Club Parade" sheet music, 1934.

"Connie's Hot Chocolates" sheet music, 1929.

fox-trot to a name band like Paul Whiteman's "on the Roof Garden" at the Biltmore Hotel; Guy Lombardo and his Royal Canadians playing the "Sweetest Music This Side of Heaven" at the Roosevelt Grill; or Dolly Dawn with her Dawn Patrol at the Taft Hotel. Between World War I and World War II, New York City alone had over a hundred hotels with "live" dance orchestras; and a host of other restaurants, ballrooms, and clubs all featured lively bands with vocalists. Even if the times were gray, "painting the town red" in Manhattan was still the rage.

As nighttime dwindled and the champagne fizzled out, the early morning "Lullaby of Broadway" party motored downtown to Greenwich Village for a taste of bohemia at "joints" like the Original Village Nut Club on Sheridan Square, the Club Howdy, or The Greenwich Village Inn. For those who had a penchant for something daring and outré a trip way uptown to jazzy Harlem was quite the thing. There was the renowned Cotton Club on Lenox Avenue and 142nd Street where Duke Ellington's or Cab Calloway's zippy bands played hot melodies like "Jungle Nights in Harlem" from *Blackberries of 1931* or "I've Got Harlem on My Mind. I've a Longing to be Lowdown . . ."; and the Savoy Ballroom offered vocalists Ella Fitzgerald and Billie Holliday, or the jumping boogie-woogie of pianist Fats Waller.

"Siboney" sheet music, 1929.

Let's Put Out the Lights and Go to Sleep

A lyric to a hit song of the Depression, introduced by Rudy Vallee and popularized by Harriet Hilliard and Ozzie Nelson, brought forth the sad lament of those with no money in the bank—asking the question—what to do about it?, and answered simply, "Let's put out the lights and go to sleep." This refrain had a special meaning to middle-class homebodies whose budgets ruled out the theatre or clubs, or who didn't live in or near a big city like New York or Chicago. When they were not at the movies, they contented themselves by staying home and reading cheap novelized versions of films or lived vicariously through periodicals purchased at the corner candy store or newsstands. These included fan and theatre magazines, detective pulp fiction, *Life, Look, Pic, The Saturday Evening Post, Time, Vanity Fair, Esquire*, and many others. Usually, Father enjoyed his favorite mystery writer, Dashiell Hammett, or potboilers by Raymond Chandler or Earl Derr Biggers while Mother preferred women's novels, such as those written by Faith Baldwin, which might use Broadway or Hollywood as a backdrop for an innocent heroine who accidentally fell into a shameful, sinful, and profligate lifestyle. If the heroine was redeemed in the end, Mother could weep happily while feeling reassured that her life as a homemaker was the most righteous path to follow. Colorful sheet music decorated the family upright piano and Sister would play and sing such favorite tunes as "Keep Your Sunny Side Up" or "Beyond the Blue Horizon . . . waits a beautiful day" while Junior read Tom Swift or The Rover Boys. Vaughn DeLeath would serenade the American family over the airwaves with her "Rock-a-Bye Parade":

Each little one with his stardust gun
Joins the Rock-a-bye Parade
And before you know
They'll go on tip-toe
where another dream is made.
So hug me tight
And put out the light
Cause you're marching unafraid
With a great big yawn
You'll toddle on . . .
In the Rock-a-Bye Parade

sweetly ending her song with a soft "Good-night . . ."

So the family members, whether tuned in to the radio, reading, sewing, or playing the piano, were often content just to be there together, safe and secure in their homes, usually retiring no later than 10:00 P.M.

Hand-embroidered winter scene, c. 1934.

The Black by Edgar Wallace, published by A. L. Burt Co., c. 1925.

Vaudeville, published by Henry Waterson, 1927.

Dashiell Hammett himself is featured on the original dust jacket for his famous mystery-detective novel *The Thin Man,* published by Grosset & Dunlap, 1933.

The Rover Boys in Camp, 1949.

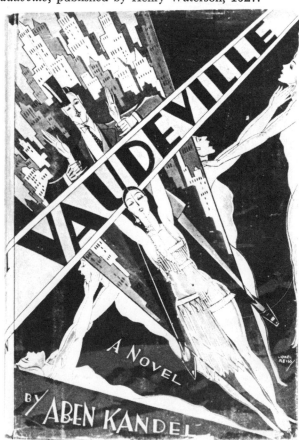

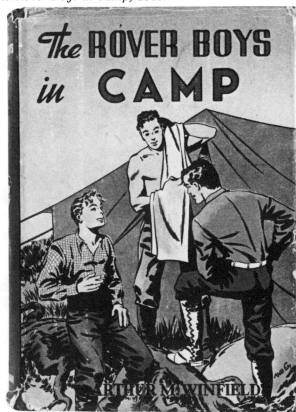

The Saturday Evening Post, January 1933.

The Saturday Evening Post, July 1934.

Bachelor magazine for the bon vivant, August 1937.

Startling Detective Adventure magazine, June 1939.

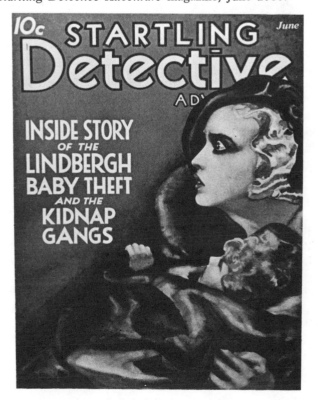

8. SODA, CIGARETTES, AND SOAP

Pop Advertising

Through the all-pervasive impact of modern media, pop advertising images have left a permanent mark on the collective consciousness of our time. Popular products drawn from the consumer culture have also been used by Pop artists who have gained wide public acceptance and critical sanction by converting the Campbell's soup can, the Brillo box, or the Coca-Cola bottle into larger-than-life icons in order to make a social statement about the world of mass production. By means of tracing and painting photoprint blowups of everyday household objects on giant canvases and through reinterpreting and developing the repetitive hard-sell techniques employed by most advertising agencies, Pop art invites the viewer to have another look at the roots of the pop idiom in our society and to perceive anew the original graphics associated with the industrial and commercial arts seen in American products.

In the sphere of advertising graphics, a group of fine-art illustrators became eminent during the early decades of the twentieth century. Rockwell Kent toiled for Sherwin-Williams Paint, Norman Rockwell created Coca-Cola calendar art, Maxfield Parrish painted his dusky, ethereal, evening-blue skies and fairy tale dream nymphs for General Electric Mazda Lamp advertisements, and J. C. Leyendecker's aristocratic young men in starched white collars became the trademark for Arrow Shirts. A. M. Cassandre travel posters and Erté covers on *Harper's Bazaar* give distinct and vivid impressions of the style of the early modern age.

Graphic symbols that were devised to create strong product identification often became permanent trademarks. The Uneeda Biscuit boy in his yellow raincoat and hat, the Morton Salt girl holding her umbrella, the Jack Frost Sugar boy, the Heinz Tomato man, Elsie the Borden cow, the Vermont Maid Syrup girl, the famous Log Cabin Syrup tin, created in the shape of an actual log cabin, the Land O' Lakes Butter Indian maiden, Droste's Dutch boy and Dutch girl having a cup of Droste's Cocoa—all have an instant association with a specific company and product.

Large, metal Coca-Cola outdoor thermometer, c. 1950.

116

namel-on-metal outdoor Coca-Cola sign, 1941.

lamorous Coca-Cola WACS on cardboard window display, 1943.

The Pause That Refreshes

Of all the American companies who advertise, none has ever been more emphatic in the use of brilliant pop graphics than the Coca-Cola Company of Atlanta, Georgia. This company created promotional campaigns literally to drive the phrase "The Pause That Refreshes" into the consumer's subconscious, programming him to order a Coke at a lunch counter.

Coca-Cola started business in 1886, and began an immediate advertising campaign, their first ad appearing on May 29 in the *Atlanta Daily Journal*. That year they sold 1,050 gallons of their syrup; and when they boosted the publicity in 1889, sales jumped up to 2,170 gallons. With an intense advertising and promotional blitz, Coca-Cola sales steadily climbed upward from 8,865 gallons in 1890 to 19,830 gallons in 1891, and to 35,360 gallons in 1892.

Key words like *refreshing, stimulating,* and *invigorating* along with "testimonials" from "doctors" were part of these initial campaigns in which Coke claimed it could act as a "nerve and brain tonic" to cure insomnia, sick headaches, indigestion, and nervous exhaustion. Because of these commercial promises, the public took to this new drink in much the same way it had embraced Moxie, which was also promoted as a popular cure-all. The early 5¢ Coke was nonalcoholic, but did use *Erythroxylon coca* plants in its original formula. The untreated leaves of this plant contain small amounts of cocaine, which, as used in the drink, provided such a minuscule amount of the drug that at least eight quarts would have to have been consumed at one sitting in order to produce delirium tremens. Drugstores sold cocaine over the counter in those happy days and doctors frequently prescribed it to their "ailing" patients. In July 1884 Sigmund Freud presented his famous "Coca" paper, outlining the evils of the drug; and by 1906 the Pure Food and Drug Act, limiting the use of opiates in food products, was passed by Congress.

Cardboard display with Pepsi-Cola cartoon cops, c. 1940.

World War II back-home "Victory Girl"
Royal Crown Cola calendar, 1944.

Anticipating the passage of this bill, the Coca-Cola Company had already treated its leaves so that no trace of the drug could be found in their concoction by government agents; but the Coca-Cola "cocaine" legend continued to persist well into the 1930s, backed up by the popular facetious expression "gimme a shot in the arm!" referring to a glass of Coke. Caffeine remained an ingredient, although it would take four six-ounce bottles of Coke to equal the effects of one cup of Maxwell House Coffee.

Coca-Cola changed its marketing procedures in 1906 and became a leisure-time refreshment instead of an elixir. Ravishing ladies were used to spur Coca-Cola sales; and the annual "Coke Girl" calendar became an institution. Lithographed-picture Coke trays featuring Pearl White, Marion Davies, and opera-singer Lillian Nordica were used by soda shops and restaurants. The company mounted a Coke advertising-product campaign, producing thousands of bottle openers, blotters, paper fans, drinking tumblers, watch fobs, and even a Tiffany-style stained-glass Coca-Cola lamp was made for ice-cream parlors.

Large chromolithographic metal signs proclaiming "Drink Coca-Cola" or "Ice-Cold Coca-Cola Sold Here" began to appear everywhere along the highways and byways, on roadside luncheonettes and

A bathing beauty displays her legs for Camels, 1949.

CAMELS
for taste and mildness!

Philip Morris's Johnny Roventini and Santa Claus trim a tree with cigarette cartons in a life-size cardboard window poster, c. 1939.

diners as well as on the exteriors and interiors of most neighborhood candy stores. A more expensive porcelain-enamel on metal process was employed to produce visually striking signs that used bold yellow and red colors to enhance the pop images of the robust, smiling, red-cheeked Coke girls or signs of the famous green hourglass-shaped bottle by itself. In the 1930s the company solicited movie stars Jean Harlow, Greta Garbo, Johnny Weissmuller, Claudette Colbert, Cary Grant, Frances Dee, and Randolph Scott to add the status and glamour of Hollywood to the Coca-Cola promotional campaigns. In 1930 Coke also introduced a life-size colorful cardboard Santa Claus created by artist Haddan Sunblom. This Santa character was well received by the public, appearing seasonally throughout the decade and into the 1940s and 1950s. The "Sprite," a boyish, Jack Frost elf with snow white-hair, perhaps a Santa's helper, wearing a Coke bottle cap for a hat, entered the advertising arena in 1946 to become synonymous with an "Ice-Cold Bottle of Coke."

Other soda companies followed much the same pattern in pop advertising graphics as Coca-Cola. These included Pepsi-Cola, Royal Crown Cola, Dr. Pepper, Spur, Canada Dry Pale Ginger Ale, Hires Root Beer, Stewart's Root Beer, Dad's Root Beer, Orange Crush, Mission Orange, Nedick's Orange, Nehi Grape and Orange, Frank's Orange Nectar, YooHoo Chocolate Drink, and 7-Up, which was originally known as a "lithiated lemon soda." Soft-drink ad signs have contributed greatly to the pop landscape of America nearly always reflecting taste, discretion, sharp graphics, and good design to sell their bubbling refreshments.

Lucky Strike Green

"Nothing lights up like a 'Lucky'"; and nothing is more a symbol for 1930s America than a clear cellophane-wrapped package of Lucky Strike Cigarettes, with its bold black lettering on a sharp red bull's-eye center outlined in gold trim against a solid forest-green background. The stark simplicity and modernity of the packaging design was a pinnacle of achievement in advertising graphics, pop Americana style. It is almost impossible to think of the madcap 1920s or the sophisticated modernity of the 1930s minus the omnipresent "green" Luckies.

In 1930 The American Tobacco Company's Lucky Strike was America's number-one smoke and led the big three in cigarettes which included R. J. Reynolds' Camels and Liggett and Myers' Chesterfield. An immense advertising budget accounted for much of the Lucky Strike lead. According to *Fortune* magazine they spent $100 million in 1936 while Chesterfield expended $90 million and Camels $70 million. In the same decade two other brands, Old Gold and Philip Morris, moved into fourth and fifth places becoming part of "the nation's big five" cigarette manufacturers.

The Lucky Strike cigarette, which originated in 1917, borrowed its name from R. A. Patterson's Lucky Strike Pipe Smoking Sliced Plug, which was registered in 1871. Much of Lucky's "modern" 1920s advertising tactics emphasized women who used cigarette smoking as the pronouncement of a new, liberated attitude for their sex. John Held, Jr.'s, drawings of skinny flappers always had a cigarette defiantly dangling from their rosebud lips; and a widely used 1928 slogan coaxed image-conscious smokers to "Reach for a Lucky Instead of a Sweet." A 1930s advertisement stated persuasively: "20,679 physicians say Luckies are less irritating"; but the most famous slogan was "L.S.M.F.T.—Lucky Strike Means Fine Tobacco." Another widely used motto—"Lucky Strike *Green* Has Gone to War"—was coined in 1942 when Lucky Strike was asked to change its green background to white for the war effort. By eliminating the solid green on the packaging, enough bronze was saved to build four hundred tanks. With this widely publicized act of patriotism by The American Tobacco Company, sales of Luckies zoomed upward thirty-eight percent.

Philip Morris made its contribution to American pop lore by engaging a tiny Hotel New Yorker bellboy named Johnny Roventini to become its primary promotional symbol. Paging in a high-pitched voice, "Call furrr Philllip Morreees," Johnny, wearing a trim gold-buttoned red-and-black uniform, a pillbox hat coupled with an ingratiating smile and apple-red cheeks, became an instant sensation on radio shows at official celebrations, and in countless advertising campaigns.

Cigarette advertisers consistently sponsored network radio shows in the 1930s. There was "The Camel Caravan" with Benny Goodman's Orchestra, which employed the oft-repeated phrase, "I'd Walk a Mile for a Camel," "The Philip Morris Playhouse," and Glenn Miller's Orchestra sponsored by Chesterfield Raleigh and Kool cigarettes both offered Tommy Dorsey and his orchestra, Old Gold had Artie Shaw and Lucky Strike presented Ben Bernie, Eddie Duchin, Kay Kayser and their orchestras, and "The Hit Parade."

Other brands that had Americans puffing smoke rings in the 1930s were Viceroy, Parliament, Marlboro (then a woman's cigarette), Herbert Tareyton, Home-Run, Pall Mall, Fatima, Spud, Wings, and the imported

Soda-pop bottles of the 1940s.

Old Dutch Cleanser cans with the original wooden packing crate, 1930s.

English Craven "A" and Player's Navy Cut, both of which used Virginia-grown tobacco. Kool, with its famous smoking penguin trademark, was an early "mentholated" cigarette that survived into the 1950s to join other new "menthol" and "low-tar" brands, "kings," and "filter-kings," which gained popularity with Americans alerted to the hazards of smoking.

Mother's Washday Blues

Monday was always the day Mother transferred the family's dirty laundry from the Pearlwick bathroom hamper into her Bendix washing machine, carefully adding the exact amount of soap powder that made the clothes sparkling clean and brighter than new. While waiting for her wash, she might dip her silk stockings, fine undies and sweaters into gentle Lux Soap, which promised to be "kinder to the hands." Once Mother finished this chore, she would scour her sink or clean the bathroom tiles with Old Dutch Cleanser, the sudsing-action powder, whose trade symbol was a Dutch girl wearing a blue dress, an apron, red wooden shoes, and a large white cap and who also "chased after dirt" with a big wood washing stick. Created in 1905, this product was Mother's

favorite, although she sometimes switched brands o impulse just to see if one cleanser really did mak things "shine brighter," as they all claimed they coul in their advertisements. Gold Dust was another scou ing powder whose brand name was also on a laundr soap. The famous black twins printed on an orang background was a familiar sight in American home for many decades. Although the Dutch girl was calle the "Goddess of household purgation," these blac babies promised they could do the job every bit a well as she. Other famous competitors in the worl of foaming-powder action were Bon Ami with its log of a newly hatched yellow chick, Bab-O, Ajax, Bab bitt's, and Sunbrite, the Sunshine Cleanser.

First in the hierarchy of soapdom was the Procte and Gamble Company whose main product, Oxydo had a box designed with concentric circles of blu and orange stripes that produced an optical illusio of movement, while promising on the reverse side t "Dissolve Dishpan Grease and Make Clothes Whiter. Lever Brothers Company was number two in Americ with its own line-up of detergents, including Rinso which claimed "Safe Rich Suds and Whiter Washes in merry advertising jingles over the radio like: "Rins White! Rinso Bright! Happy little wash-day song!, Sunny Monday, Sunlight Soap, Welcome Soap, Gol Dust, Fairy Soap, and the renowned Lux which wa recommended by famous Hollywood stars who als "drank Coca-Cola" and "smoked Lucky Strike Green just like everyone else. Lever Brothers also brough out a kitchen product called Spry, a vegetable shorten ing, to compete with Procter and Gamble's Crisco but the company's main concern and purpose, a stated by Lever Brothers President Francis A. Count way, who by earning a salary of $469,700 in the yea 1939 became the highest paid industrial executive i the United States (outside of Hollywood), were: "Th pleasure and *profit* to be derived from keeping a dirt world clean in the future" (*Fortune*, November 1940)

Sears, Roebuck and Co. ad for a Kenmore washing ma chine with hand wringer, 1931.

No doubt about it, Mother loved soap, or at least gave the hearty appearance of loving it, always beaming, humming, and singing as she hung her damp clothes out on the line every sunny Monday morning; birds would surround her, cheerfully chirping for their share of bread crumbs, as the soft female voices and droll sounds of organ music—from a radio soap opera —were heard throughout the house.

And what did Mother do after she was done with her Monday washday products—Lux, Ivory Snow, Tide, Duz, or Super Suds? Perhaps she took a well-earned rest period over a cup of A&P, freshly perked, Eight O'Clock Coffee while munching one of her own delicious homemade doughnuts, which she had deep-fried in Crisco or Spry the night before. Maybe she pondered family meals, anxiously attempting to balance her weekly shopping list with her Depression household food budget. But somehow if the clothes hanging on the line were becoming whiter and brighter each Monday—through the "miracle of modern washday products"—that was all that really mattered.

Original soapboxes of the 1940s.

INDEX

Page references for illustrations are in **boldface** type.